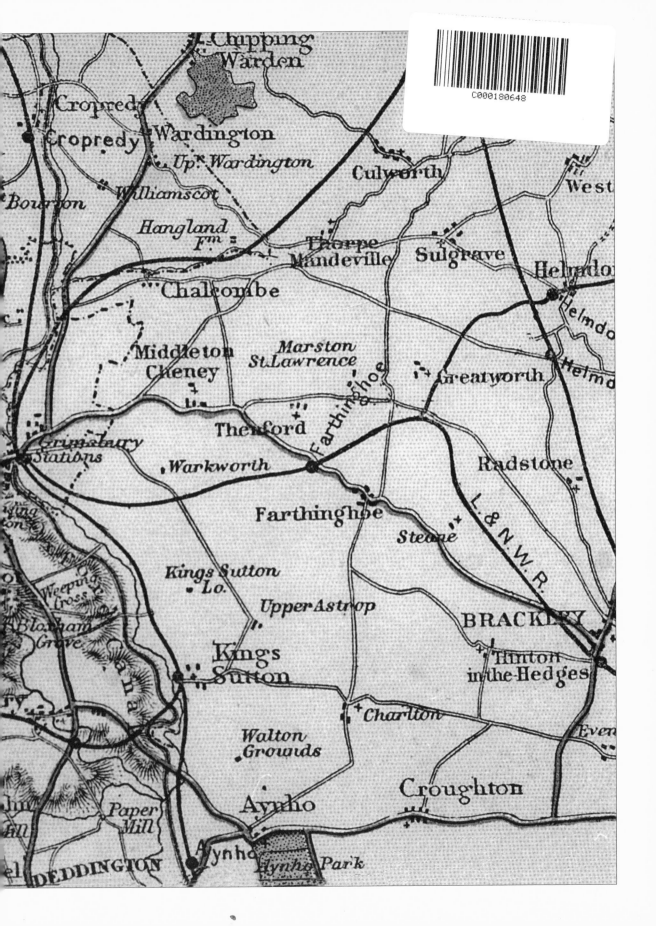

BANBURY

A HISTORY

Banbury Cross

BANBURY
A HISTORY

BRIAN LITTLE

Phillimore

2003

Published by
PHILLIMORE & CO. LTD
Shopwyke Manor Barn, Chichester, West Sussex, England

ISBN 1 86077 242 0

Printed and bound in Great Britain by
THE CROMWELL PRESS
Trowbridge, Wiltshire

CONTENTS

List of Illustrations

Frontispiece: Banbury Cross

ACKNOWLEDGEMENTS

Aerofilms Limited, 118; *Banbury Guardian* newspaper, 7, 14, 25, 26, 27, 28, 30, 31, 35, 37, 42, 43, 56, 119, 133; Banbury Historical Society, 1, 2, 11, 12, 13, 22, 34, 41, 51; Banbury School, 18, 126; Banburyshire Study Centre, 45; Birmingham University Field Archaeology Unit, 8, 9, 10, 20, 24, 69; Blinkhorns, 107, 113, 121, 145; Kraft Foods UK Ltd & Frank Toole, 120, 129; Oxfordshire County Council, 137, 138; John Ashworth, 151; John Batts, 123, 124; Helen Brooks, 108; John Brooks, 99; June Charles, 113; Chris Cooper, 100; Jean Davis, 110; John Dossett Davies, 94; Doreen Essex, 115, 116; Neithrop Felons, 54; Peggy Gilbert, 105; Jenny Glyn, 47; Sean Haggar, 127; June Hardie, 74; Malcolm Hearn, 109; Pauline McTimony, 82; Rod Prewer, 142, 143; Harry Rhodes, 111, 122, 148; the late Mrs Truss, 96.

Thanks also to Martin Allitt of the Banburyshire Study Centre of Banbury Library, Chris Day of Banbury Museum, Jeremy Gibson of the Banbury Historical Society and to the staff of F-Stop Photography and Banbury Colour Imaging.

I am especially indebted to Stephen Litherland of Birmingham University Field Archaeology Unit and to Professor Brian Goodey of Oxford Brookes University for their collaboration in the production of this book. In particular my sincere thanks must go to Margaret Little, my wife, for kindly word processing the manuscript and offering a sounding board at all times.

INTRODUCTION

Banbury is a Cherwell valley town in the north of Oxfordshire. It is about 23 miles to the north of the city of Oxford and close to the administrative boundaries of Northamptonshire and Warwickshire.

A bridge across the River Cherwell separates Banbury and Grimsbury, which existed as two separate hamlets in Saxon times. Recent archaeological investigations have revealed a late-Saxon manor house on the same site as Banbury Castle.

In the 12th century, Alexander, Bishop of Lincoln, laid out a planned new town that incorporated a Market Place and was protected by the second in a sequence of castles. His granting of a market charter launched Banbury on its history as a regional centre for the buying and selling of livestock and goods. This function remained unchallenged until the dramatic closure of the 'Stockyard of Europe' in 1998.

Recently a new shopping mall called Castle Quay has developed close to the Market Place and nearby Bridge Street. This has shifted the town's commercial heart eastwards and away from the pattern of medieval streets which down the centuries have attracted people to a place of family businesses.

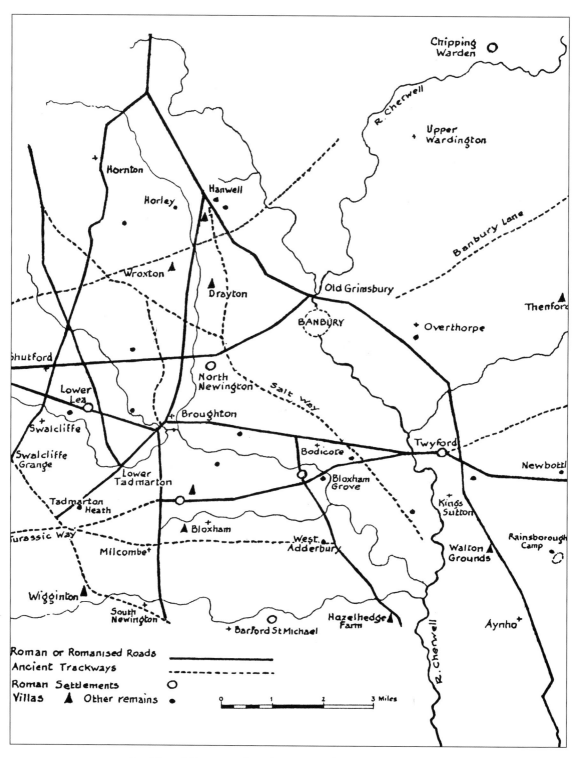

1 *Map of Roman roads and ancient trackways around Banbury.*

One

Emergent Banbury

Banbury lies at the heart of an informal region known locally as Banburyshire.[1] This stretches from Edge Hill to Deddington and from Chipping Norton towards Brackley in Northamptonshire (see endpapers). Much of the area is characterised by red soils, warm brown stone buildings and a fair proportion of thatched roofs. These Redlands are Liassic territory of limestone and clays.[2] The period of their formation was warm and wet, probably sub-tropical. Forests abounded near shallow seas and their fossilised remains are locked into rock strata, especially in the Wroxton area. The seas contained many animal organisms such as huge snails known as ammonites. Their shelly remains occur widely and especially in quarries and other excavations.[3]

Prehistoric finds and sites have not been abundant in Banburyshire. The Palaeolithic (Stone Age) and Mesolithic periods saw much greater human activity on the drier uplands further south and within the Thames river gravels. Neolithic times brought movement closer to our area but there have been few finds to match the 1991 discovery of a shafted blade saw on a site close to the Middleton Cheney bypass just to the east of Banbury.

Locally the Bronze Age is represented by discoveries such as a concentration of axes at the former Chipping Warden aerodrome. These were found when they passed through a potato-sorting machine. It is likely that they were left by itinerant smiths who we know entered southern Britain round about 1000 B.C. The Iron Age was altogether a busier time and this has been confirmed by the archaeology of hill-forts such as Madmarston near Swalcliffe.

A map of prehistoric and Roman trackways of the Banbury district reveals an intensive network that was conditioned by factors of geology, drainage, commodity movements and military operations. Prehistoric ways followed the dry uplands and avoided the wide and wet river valleys such as the Cherwell Valley where crossings were few. Typical of these routes were the Jurassic Way that connected Bath with Lincoln and the Port Way that intersected it on a north to south alignment.

In the broadest sense, the frame of the area is set by a great triangle of Roman roads comprising the Fosse Way, Watling Street and Akeman Street, but the Romans needed not only great military roads but also local roads for general communications, and some of these developed out of the ancient trackways such as the Port Way. Banburyshire is not short of Romano-British remains. Within the bounds of the parish, traces of a substantial Roman building at Wykham Park, lots of potsherds and finds of coins near Banbury Castle and in the gardens of houses in the town clearly demonstrate a wealth of activity. Yet there was no urban settlement.

An important ancient trackway is the road we now call Banbury Lane, which originated from near Northampton and entered the

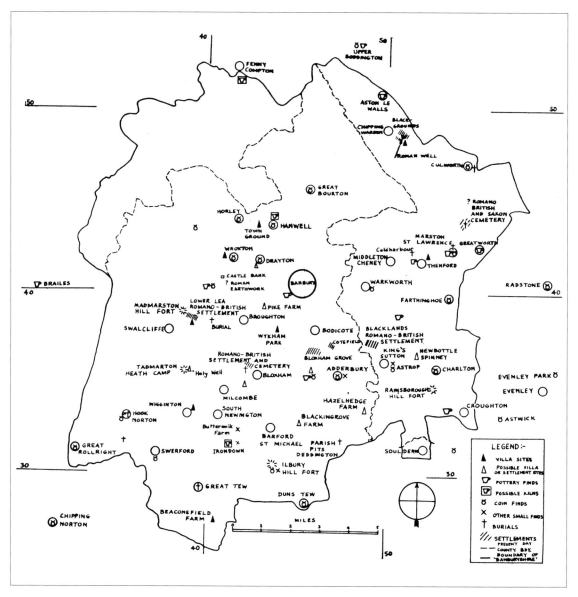

2   *Map of Roman Banburyshire.*

Banbury district close to Middleton Cheney. In the second half of the fifth century a Saxon incursion from East Anglia exploited this route. Danish invaders came by the same road in the year 913 and laid waste the land all the way westwards to Hook Norton. On a more constructive note, Banbury's Market Place was shaped in the typical leg-of-mutton Danish style.

Banbury itself grew up on the margins of the Cherwell valley. The original site of its castle was a knoll of well-drained gravels above the blue Lias clays. This was also a dry point for prehistoric man, as evidenced by discoveries of flint flakes and implements during archaeological investigations. Development had to wait until Saxon times, when it has been postulated

3 *Thenford Way was an ancient route into Banburyshire.*

Banesberie and Grimsberie were hamlets on either side of the River Cherwell. The latter name encompasses a pseudonym of Woden, the Nordic god, and this may be considered an indication that settlement at Grimsberie was earlier than that at Banesberie. However, despite phases of archaeology directed by Fasham, Rodwell and Litherland no clear evidence of Saxon settlement has come to light in either location. It seems highly likely that any Saxon habitation was destroyed by later periods of development. In any case, wattle and daub structures would have been ephemeral and no archaeological evidence has been found for a Saxon minster, which would have been built in stone.

A rescue dig in the late 1980s close to Hennef Way (link road to the M40) produced a small quantity of pottery from ditches beneath the ridge and furrow west of Grimsbury Green Road. This included St Neots ware and a few contemporary fabrics suggesting this may have been part of the late Saxon settlement mentioned in Domesday. Recently, further exploration in this area has focused on prehistoric activity but the results will not be known for some time.[4]

Banesberie could have been just west of the Cherwell bridging point. Here was the opportunity to be on the dry side of a river cliff. The only other feasible site is close by the Manor of Calthorpe near where the north-south and east-west roads cross. Trenches dug during archaeological investigations prior to the opening of the first Sainsbury's store in Banbury revealed only medieval pottery.[5]

Previous histories of Banbury failed to address the issue of these hamlets. Both Beesley (1841) and Potts (1958) offer only general accounts of Saxon England. It was left to Dr E.R.C. Brinkworth, in a short popular history

4 *Roman coins found in the Banbury area.*   **5** *Roman pottery and artefacts of Banburyshire.*

of the town written in the 1950s,[6] to comment that 'the origin of Banbury as of most old towns, is obscure'. However he did not have the benefit of later archaeological reports. Some indication of Saxon Banbury became apparent during Birmingham University 1998 field operations that took place in two locations, namely the Castle Precinct and the triangular area bounded by Bridge Street and Mill Lane, which was on the eastern fringe of the Market Place.

The first phase of occupation in the Castle Precinct area has been dated late Saxon/Early Norman. It appears that a site was cleared for a timber castle. The earliest defensive remains of this consisted of a ditch aligned east to west and measuring ten metres in width and three metres

in depth. This could have been part of a moated enclosure but evidence for a southerly return of this ditch was not conclusive. However beam slots for a timber rampart were apparent on the inner margin where material had been dumped to create more of a defensive obstacle.

The main late Saxon/early Norman feature within the Bridge Street/Mill Lane zone of investigation was again a ditch also orientated east to west. It is thought that this feature had a very different function from the castle mound ditch. The consensus of opinion was that it was an early field boundary linking a tributary stream known as the Cuttle Brook with the River Cherwell. It was found to contain Saxo-Norman pottery, but perhaps of greater significance was

ROMAN PAVEMENT AT WIGGINTON

6 *Roman pavements near Banbury.*

7 *The castle knoll as seen from the Grimsbury side of the Oxford Canal.*

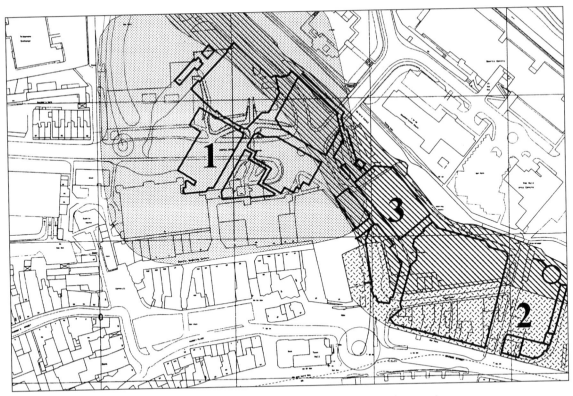

8   *Zones of archaeological response (scale: 100m grid-squares).*

Phase	Description	Zone 1	Zone 2	Zone3
0	PRE-SAXON	X		
1	LATE-SAXON/EARLY NORMAN	X	X	
1a	Timber Castle	X		
1b	Restructuring of the timber Castle	X		
2	1150-1250 PLANNED TOWN	X	X	X
3	1250-1640 MATURING MARKET TOWN	X	X	X
4	CIVIL WAR	X	X	X
4a	Refortification	X		X
4b	Demolition of the Castle	X		
4c	Reconstruction of the town in the aftermath of the war		X	
5	1778 IMPACT OF THE CANAL	X	X	X
6	LATER VICTORIAN IMPROVEMENTS	X	X	X
7	20th CENTURY	X	X	X

9   *Table giving summary of archaeological evidence.*

10 *Excavation of the backfilled moat of the earliest Saxo-Norman castle.*

the alignment of Mill Lane with this ditch. The lane was a medieval development designed to link the 12th-century Market Place with the bishop's mill to the east of the town.

From documentary evidence we learn that at some time after St Birinus' mission to Wessex and the foundation of his see at Dorchester-on-Thames in 634, the Bishop of Dorchester had extensive estates in north Oxfordshire that included Banbury. When Remigius, the first Norman bishop, removed the see from Dorchester to Lincoln, the bishops of Lincoln became lords of the manor of Banbury, as tenants-in-chief of the king in return for military service, as was the Norman custom, and by 1086 Banbury was one of the administrative centres of the bishop's estates. This was acknowledged in the survey of 1082 and included in Domesday Book a few years later.

A translation of the Domesday entry printed in Beesley's *The History of Banbury* says that 'The Bishop himself holds Banesberie. There are 50 hides [aproximately 5,000 acres] there. Of these the Bishop has, in the demesne [the part of the manor which the lord keeps for his own use] land to 10 ploughs, and 3 hides besides the inland … In King Edward's [the Confessor] time, there were 33 ploughs and a half; and Bishop Remigius found the same number.'[7]

There is no evidence that William the Conqueror visited Banbury. Shortly after the Conquest he came to Wallingford and later was in Oxford. A local legend has it that he slept in the *Altarstone Inn* in Banbury, which was next to the *Old George* (now Barclays Bank). If this is so then mention of this inn in Corporation accounts of 1596/7 may not be the earliest reference to it.[8]

Two

Castles and Church
1100 to 1500

Undoubtedly the most notable bishop of Lincoln as far as Banbury is concerned was Alexander de Blois, who was consecrated in 1123. His small stature belied an agile mind and an inclination to live in splendour, which led to his being styled the 'Magnificent'. Geoffrey of Monmouth dedicated part of his history of the Britons to Alexander, 'a prelate of the greatest piety and wisdom. There is no one among the clergy or the laity attended with such a train of knights and nobles whom his established piety and great munificence engaged in his service.'[1]

The evolution of the Market Place appears to have taken place as an outcome of the activities of Alexander. The building of the castle, the coming together of land routes and the possible use of the River Cherwell for trade, combined with the great agricultural wealth of the area surrounding Banbury, provided every incentive for a planned new town with a large Market Place. The Normans brought with them a new class of tenant, the 'burgage tenure' holders who held their tenure in exchange for money rents rather than service. Markets were the retail trade centres of the day, the place where people came together to buy and sell goods, and shops at this time tended to be small booths or workshops where items could be ordered and made. It is also thought that Alexander was responsible for the building of the old St Mary's Church.

Alexander the Magnificent needed to protect his town. This he did by enlarging the Saxo-Norman defended enclosure, excavating a new moat and constructing a complex of ironstone buildings. One of these structures appears to have been two storeys high and a quality development, possibly a hall that would have had ancillary buildings. The guiding principle behind this and a later castle appears to have been the need to offer protection towards the south. On the northern boundary a marsh acted as a natural defence.

Alexander was a renowned castle builder and this may have alarmed King Stephen who was anxious to have control of all fortified places at a time when his right to the throne was being challenged by the Empress Maud, daughter of the previous king, Henry I. At midsummer 1139 the king summoned Bishop Roger of Salisbury, who had recently fortified his castle at Devizes, and was Alexander's uncle (gossip said father) and patron, to his court at Oxford. Roger, being suspicious of the king's motives, persuaded Alexander and another 'clerical nephew', Nigel, Bishop of Ely, to accompany him. A quarrel at court led to the arrest of Alexander and Roger (Nigel escaped capture). Alexander was imprisoned at Newark for a period of seven months, during which time he was forced to surrender his castles and lands to the king. However, as far as we can tell, this did not lead to military action at Banbury and Alexander recovered his castles soon after his release.

As the market town matured so the degree of fortification came to suggest a primary urban

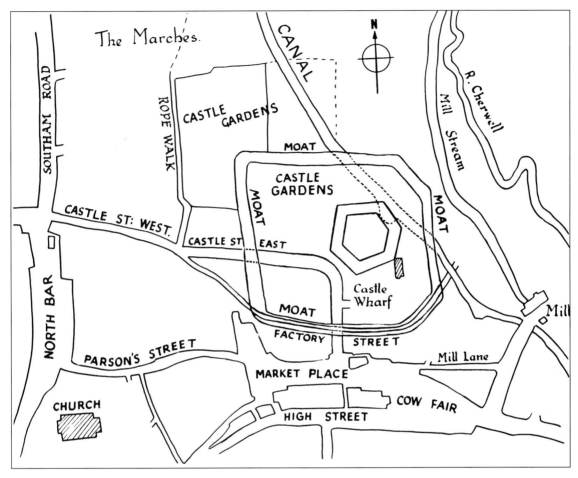

11   *The castle in relation to the Market Place.*

castle that reflected confidence in the medieval town layout. The demolition of Alexander's castle and its replacement by a concentric double-ditched structure has been dated to a period from the mid-13th to the 14th centuries. Archaeological investigation in 1998 revealed that the key feature of the new stone castle was a circular building that reflected principles of military architecture largely based on crusader castles. Possibly this was a chapel.[2] The greatly expanded castle had two moats. An inner one appears to have been re-cut several times, finally and most significantly during the 17th-century Civil War. An outer moat was at least three metres deep but may have been an even more formidable feature.

From William the Conqueror onwards kings of England endeavoured to establish royal control over the church. In particular, the right of presenting the parson, especially when the appointment went to a foreign ecclesiastic, and the collection of taxes were areas of dispute. On 28 April 1139 an instrument from Pope Innocent II to Alexander stated that the church and all its possession should be under the special protection of the Holy See, and mentions Banbury among those possessions. In 1337 a dispute arose over the Prebend of Banbury.

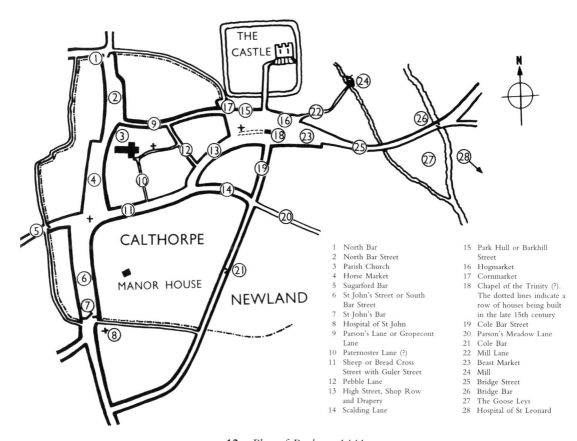

THE CASTLE

CALTHORPE

MANOR HOUSE

NEWLAND

1 North Bar
2 North Bar Street
3 Parish Church
4 Horse Market
5 Sugarford Bar
6 St John's Street or South
    Bar Street
7 St John's Bar
8 Hospital of St John
9 Parson's Lane or Gropecont
    Lane
10 Paternoster Lane (?)
11 Sheep or Bread Cross
    Street with Guler Street
12 Pebble Lane
13 High Street, Shop Row
    and Drapery
14 Scalding Lane

15 Park Hull or Barkhill
    Street
16 Hogmarket
17 Cornmarket
18 Chapel of the Trinity (?).
    The dotted lines indicate a
    row of houses being built
    in the late 15th century
19 Cole Bar Street
20 Parson's Meadow Lane
21 Cole Bar
22 Mill Lane
23 Beast Market
24 Mill
25 Bridge Street
26 Bridge Bar
27 The Goose Leys
28 Hospital of St Leonard

12   *Plan of Banbury 1441.*

Edward III had appointed Paul de Montefiore but another prebendary had been name by Pope Benedict XI. On this occasion Edward's nominee stood down and the papal appointment was confirmed. Edward was firmer in his stand against the collection of taxes by foreign clergy and tried to forbid them from setting foot in the country.[3]

At times of interregnum in the bishopric of Lincoln, the king would assume responsibility for the bishop's lands. However, this was not the case in 1321 when Edward II seized the castle and the bishop's lands. The cause was an armed revolt against the king led by Thomas, Duke of Lancaster, supported by the then bishop, Henry Burgherst. Also involved was Robert de Stoke of Wykham, who had charge of Banbury

castle. Responsibility for the castle passed to Robert de Arden. Robert lived at Drayton and it seems he acquired Wykham, which was in the parish of Banbury, after the fall of Robert de Stoke. He was a powerful man, knight of the shire for Oxford and more importantly a commissioner for arraying the combined forces of Oxfordshire and Berkshire. Under him the castle was put in readiness to withstand a rebel attack but none came.

The existence of a stone bridge across the River Cherwell appears to date from about 1294. At the Banbury end were arches spanning the mill stream which powered the Bishop of Lincoln's grain mill. Responsibility for the repair of this bridge and the accompanying highway seems to have been vested in appointees of the

13 *The stone bridge which spanned the River Cherwell.*

Corporation called bridgemasters, whose duty it was to administer the town's charities. They were dependent on income from rents on burgages located in the near vicinity. Evidence for these at a later date is contained in the 'Decree of the Commissioners of Charitable Uses' dated 1603. For instance, there was a burgage on the south side of Bridge End Street that brought in an annual rent of 2s. 6d., and this was used to pay for repair work. Until the late 19th century the eastern end of the bridge over the Cherwell marked the eastern boundary of the borough as Grimsbury, although part of the ecclesiastical parish of Banbury, was in Northamptonshire.

The town had not expanded since the mid-13th century addition of Newland on the southern side of the medieval core. The name 'Newland' usually referred to a new area opened up to fresh burgage tenants. Part of the explanation for the lack of further expansion may be a reduction in population possibly due to plague. Prosperity also declined and this was reflected in property costs prior to the rental of 1441. After this date there was an upswing in the economy based on local products. Banbury was noted for cheese, and Shakespeare was to use the expression 'he was as slender as a Banbury cheese' confident that playgoers would understand his meaning. In the 15th century Banbury became recognised as a wool collecting centre for the south Midlands. Above all, however, a successful farming hinterland depended on Banbury as its logical Market Place.

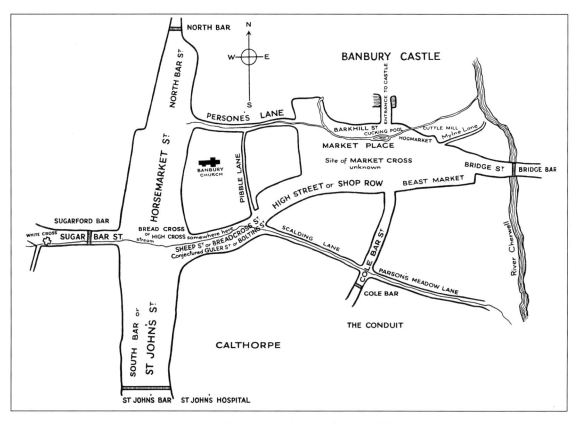

14   *Streets of Banbury at the end of the Middle Ages.*

It is possible, though we have no references to it, that Banbury had a Saxon minster on the site adjoining the Horse Fair that was chosen by Bishop Alexander of Lincoln for the predecessor of the present building. The prime evidence we have for dating the church to the time of Bishop Alexander is a drawing and description of the rounded arches and circular piers of the nave that are typical features of Norman architecture. It is fortunate that these had survived until the time of the church's demolition in 1790. The church had been much altered and enlarged in response to the growth of population and the evolution of artistic ideas and building skills during the later Middle Ages. In particular, aisles had been added in the 13th century, the transepts enlarged in the mid-14th century, and a clerestory built. The two transepts

contained side chapels, the southern one of which was dedicated to the Virgin Mary and served as the Chantry Chapel of the Guild of St Mary. The dedication of the other chapel is not known.

Next to the parish church, the most important religious organisation in Banbury was the Charity of St Mary founded in 1413. Johnson (page 51) records that Henry V granted to the prebendary of Banbury, on payment of 20 marks, the right to use a donation of land 'twelve messuages and a moiety of a virgate of land' in Banbury, Wickham and Neithrop made by Richard of Eton, William Harris, John Warr, John of Towcester and John Danvers of Calthorpe House to maintain two chaplains. The chaplains were to say mass in the parish church of Banbury 'for the good estate of the

15   The former St Mary's Church with its fine tower and south chapel.

16   Ground plan of the former St Mary's Church.

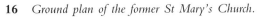

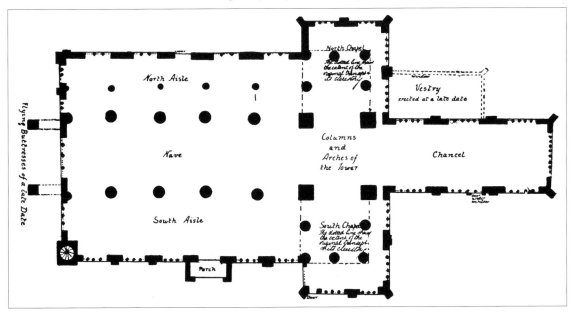

NORMAN CORBEL HEAD.

KING'S HEAD.

GROTESQUE FIGURE.

HEAD OF CHANCEL DOOR.

GURGOYLE.

WINDOW HEAD.
(Probably from Clerestory of Nave.)

EFFIGY OF AN ECCLESIASTIC.
(Now in the Churchyard.)

ARCH AND SPANDRELS.

17   *Remains of former church.*

TRACERY OF WINDOW.
(14th Cent.)

NICHE AND CANOPY.
(15th Cent.)

STONE PANELLING. *(15th Cent.)*

STONE PANELLING. *(15th Cent.)*

King, the Bishops of Winchester and Lincoln, of the Prebendary and the grantors and of their souls after death'. In 1448 Henry VI, at the cost of another 20 marks, granted a charter for a Guild to take over the Chantry. At this time the number of chaplains was increased to three and the Guild supported eight poor people in an almshouse. The Guild acquired property all over the town and became very wealthy by the time of the Dissolution. The wealth enabled it to support 12 people in the almshouse rather than the original eight. Interestingly, much later, in 1548, a charity was set up in Grimsbury with lands worth an annual sum of £3 6s. 8d. but an air of mystery surrounds both the benefactor and the purpose of the charity.[4]

An especially striking feature of the old church was its Perpendicular tower built in the mid-15th century to replace an earlier Norman one. This second tower had two storeys and very striking buttresses. The 18th-century antiquarian Dr Stukeley observed in 1712 that the tower had been higher at a previous stage but Potts doubted this. A more likely explanation was that the top of the tower had been damaged in the Civil War and part of it pulled down before restoration. Housed in the tower were six bells cast by the Bagleys at Chacombe.[5]

Little information is available on how the church was furnished. There was a carved timber chancel screen and an organ purchased by voluntary subscription in 1760. The font was octagonal in the early Decorated style and dated to the year 1320. It now occupies the south-east corner of the churchyard being out of keeping with the classical style of the new building.

A number of documentary sources make reference to the prebendary. Banbury was a prebend in Lincoln Cathedral. A prebend was the stipend assigned to a canon or member of the cathedral chapter who had a stall there. From Norman times it was the custom for the chapter of Lincoln Cathedral to recite the whole book of psalms daily. At the time of Bishop Hugh Wells (1209-35) the psalms allocated to the Banbury prebend were 81st, 82nd, 83rd and 84th. The last of these contains the words of the borough motto: 'For the Lord God is a sun and a shield'.

Very early on, the essential work of the parish and the spiritual needs of the parishioners were taken care of by a succession of vicars, and the collection of tithes and management of property by an official. For although the duties at Lincoln Cathedral took up only a small part of the prebendary's time, he would not necessarily spend much of it in Banbury. Many prebendaries held

other offices. At the time of Alexander's predecessor, William Rufus' chancellor, Robert Bloet (1094-1123), the bishop who gave all the greater and lesser tithes of Banbury to Eynsham Abbey, there appears not to have been a prebend of Banbury and so it is possible that the position dated from the building of the church. The first prebendary we know the name of is John de Giles, recorded as holding it in 1231-2. The exact date of the establishment of the vicarage is equally hazy. Potts was unable to trace a vicar earlier than a man called Roger who died in 1278.

An important religious building in the town was the Hospital of St John the Baptist that was founded in the early 13th century and stood outside the St John's Bar (South Bar). It was well endowed, the prior holding eight burgages in Banbury in 1225 and later bequests including Wykham Mill. These hospitals were modelled on the infirmaries set up in Jerusalem by the Knights Hospitallers of St John of Jerusalem but the Banbury one was firmly under the control

18 *St John's Hospital at the South Bar.*

of the Bishop of Lincoln. The hospital tended the sick, looked after travellers and provided some care for the poor. It came to an end in 1549 as a result of an Act of 1547 that dissolved chantries and the buildings were sold to Thomas Hawkins.

The hospital housed a free grammar school for 16 scholars, the first Banbury Grammar School. The most celebrated master was John Stanbridge who held the appointment until his death in 1510 and wrote the famous 'Stanbridge Grammar'. Under John the school acquired a great reputation for the quality of its teaching.

During the 14th and 15th centuries the town became indelibly associated with fairs and markets. In 1328 an account of Pavage in Banbury reveals the varying values of items sold. Every quarter of corn for sale was worth one farthing, whereas a horseload of cloth fetched one halfpenny. The first mention we have of a fair is in a charter of Henry II granting an annual occasion for Whitsun week. In 1329 Bishop Henry petitioned Edward II for an extension of his two fairs in Banbury. A new charter gave the right to two eight-day fairs, one starting on Ascension Day and the other on the Thursday after Whitsun. Fairs in the 13th century attracted people from a much wider area than markets and were very important to the merchants and traders.

Development of a late medieval built up area to the east of the original Market Place has been revealed by excavations within the Mill Lane/Bridge Street triangle. The first buildings along the Mill Lane frontage date to the 1500s, sections of ironstone walls belonging to these being revealed. It appears that Bridge Street had similar structures, as evidenced by the nature of a plot site at the junction of Mill Street and Bridge Street. A rental of 1441 confirms the concentration of properties here. Thirty-seven are recorded as fronting Bridge Street, which itself receives a first specific mention in 1393.[6]

In this area the west to east course of the Cuttle Brook is cited as a boundary to the Market Place related settlement. Excavation of silty clays, which mark the course it followed to the Cherwell, suggest this water course was a substantial feature, some three metres wide and three metres deep. A factor in its physical character was that it gathered water from several ditches. The discovery of two inter-connected ditches with a sequence of post holes just to the north of the brook may provide evidence for a riverside wharf. By contrast a large east-west channel below what used to be Factory Street is likely to have been an outlet to the river from the outer castle moat.

19 *The South or St John's Bar.*

20 *Excavation of medieval ironstone building foundations fronting Mill Lane.*

Archaeological excavations have also helped to achieve a clearer understanding of medieval Old Grimsbury. Encouraged by an evaluation report of 1993, the Oxford Archaeological Unit carried out an area excavation at Manor Farm in August 1998. Old Grimsbury lies to the east of the River Cherwell. Geologically it consists of poorly drained alluvial clays. At the time of the 1998 investigation the site was a surviving pocket of pasture called Square Close in the 1852 Tithe Award.

An important element in the pattern of settlement is the manor of Grimsbury. At the time of Domesday it was assessed at six ploughlands, 30 acres of meadow and a mill. From the 13th century until the Dissolution of the Monasteries in 1538, there were two manors. In 1315 the then owner granted his land to the Prior and Canons of Bicester Priory and members of the Bottiler family. At that time the Prior of Bicester had in his possession one messuage, ten acres of arable land, four acres of meadow and rent amounting to a yearly sum of 25s. In 1330 this grant was confirmed by John Bottiler and Beatrice, his wife, who were in possession of the other manor. Beatrice was a descendant of Thomas de Park who was

responsible for the original division of the land.

Manor lands may or may not have been included in the 1998 study but there are no such doubts about the great late medieval expansion of sheep farming, which meant that Grimsbury's pastureland supported very large flocks. The area became a focus for enclosures. Unsurprisingly, an early case was brought under an Act of 1536 that sought to return enclosed pastureland to the plough.

The main finds revealed by the 1998 excavations were pottery and sheep bones. The latter combined with documentary evidence make it certain that Grimsbury and nearby Nethercot were dominated by sheep farming in late medieval times. Depopulation was a related problem. Associated with this trend was the late 15th-century/early 16th-century demolition of buildings. However, Manor Road Farm was not a replacement for occupied buildings. It is more likely that the present farm is a rebuild of a late medieval predecessor on the same site.[7]

The second half of the 15th century saw the struggle between the royal houses of Lancaster and York for the English crown which ended with the death of Richard III on Bosworth Field. The decisive actions that

21 *Grimsbury Manor House in 1999 before restoration.*

comprised this struggle missed this part of the country. However, in July 1469, eight years after the supporters of Edward, Duke of York, had proclaimed him King Edward IV, a popular rising broke out in Yorkshire and the rebel forces proceeded towards London. The Earl of Pembroke with a royal army of many thousands of Welshmen had met up with Lord Stafford and a body of 6,000 'good archers' raised in Somerset and Devon, and whilst in the Banbury area, they received intelligence that the rebel forces were marching towards Northampton. They discovered the rebels at Edgcote. Leaving the Welshmen camped at Wardon Hill (Chipping Warden), on 23 July Stafford and Pembroke set up quarters in Banbury and on the following two days there were minor skirmishes. On 25 July a quarrel broke out between the two leaders over lodgings, which resulted in Lord Stafford 'in great dispite' promptly departing with his whole company in the direction of Chipping Norton, thus leaving the Earl of Pembroke's troops without archers. In the evening the Welshmen were attacked by a small force of rebels led by Sir Henry Neville, who was captured and killed. The next day the main body of the rebel army attacked the royal forces and a fierce battle was fought on the plain known as Danesmoor near Trafford Bridge. For a while things were evenly matched but went the way of the rebels after they were strengthened by the arrival of Northamptonshire sympathisers under John Clapham. Pembroke's forces were reduced to a 'disorganised and flying rabble' which fled towards Banbury and rushed through its streets. The Earl of Pembroke and other leaders were captured and later executed close by St Mary's Church. Nor did Lord Stafford escape. King Edward directed the sheriffs of Somerset and Devonshire to apprehend him and he was beheaded at Bridgwater for his traitorous act.

Three

TUDOR BANBURY
1500 TO 1603

The mid-16th century was something of a watershed in the way Banbury was governed. From this time onwards the townspeople had some say in the way the town was run.

During the reign of Henry VIII the long struggle between the crown and the papacy for control of church appointments, and the right to have legal matters concerning Englishmen decided in England, came to a head over the matter of Henry's divorce from Queen Catherine of Aragon. In Tudor times the rulers of the English Church were all royal appointees mostly serving the crown as ministers, ambassadors and civil servants. Bishops, in particular, drew their pay from the church but earned it in the service of the crown. An outstanding example is Thomas Wolsey, later Cardinal, who was briefly Bishop of Lincoln and Lord of Banbury in 1514 before being translated to the archbishopric of York. Pushing a series of Acts through a somewhat reluctant Parliament, Henry broke away from the Church of Rome and established the Church of England and declared himself its supreme governor.

After his break with Rome Henry VIII instituted two great inquests into monastic habits and into church revenues from manors, land and tithes. The latter is contained in the *Valor Ecclesiasticus* and includes details of revenues from all the property and tithes owned by the bishopric of Lincoln in Banbury, as well as those belonging to the Hospital of St John and the Guild of the Blessed Mary. A transcript of those

parts concerning the Banbury district provides a window on some of the leading personalities of the day. Anthony Cope of Grimsbury Manor had property that included several mills amongst his profitable enterprises. Banbury's William Fletcher paid 10s. 0d. for a cottage in Shop Row, which was situated where the High Street met Cole Bar Street (Broad Street).

The break with Lincoln came a few years later in 1542, when Henry created the diocese of Oxford, and the Banbury prebend ceased to exist six years later. Banbury remained exempt from the jurisdiction of the new diocese because of its former status as a 'peculiar' under the Dean and Chapter of Lincoln. It owed its status as peculiar, or exempt jurisdiction, to Robert de Chesney, who was Bishop of Lincoln from 1148 to 1155. He had decreed that all the prebendal parishes within his diocese, of which Banbury was one, were exempt from his jurisdiction and that of his archdeacon. The jurisdiction of the Peculiar Court of Banbury extended into many adjacent rural parishes in both Oxfordshire and Northamptonshire. Despite representations from the diocese of Oxford over succeeding centuries, Lincoln's jurisdiction continued until 1846, when all peculiars were abolished. The main advantage to the parishioners of Banbury's peculiar status was that the Court of the Peculiar met in Banbury, usually in the parish church of St Mary's. These ecclesiastical courts ruled on many areas of life such as the proving of wills,

22 *The area covered by the Peculiar of Banbury.*

William Cornwell on a 21-year lease. When this expired they passed into the hands of the Bishop of Oxford.

By the time of the Reformation, much of Parsons Street had become Church property. From the western end as far as and including Church Lane and Church Passage the land was prebendal and was specifically used to redeem the Bishop of Oxford's land tax.[1] By contrast, properties on the north side of Parsons Street were used to raise money for the repair of the church. Other adjoining land including the Marches was termed prebendal but was sold separately.[2]

matrimonial cases and sexual offences such as adultery, whoredom, incest and bastardy as well as disputes over tithes.

The secular results of the Reformation led to the surrender of the manor and castle to Edward VI in 1547 by Henry Holbech. Shortly after this date the manor was held by the Duke of Somerset, the Lord Protector, who passed all the property in Banbury that had belonged to the bishops of Lincoln to John Dudley, Earl of Warwick, who was created Duke of Northumberland in 1551. The prebendal estate also became part of the possessions of the Duke of Northumberland who sold it, together with the manor, castle and hundred of Banbury, to the king. In the reign of Queen Elizabeth I these lands were leased to the Fiennes family but the rectory and the advowson went to a

In the mid–16th century Banbury was in the midst of a transition from the old medieval system of government, directed and controlled by the Bishop of Lincoln or the crown, to a free corporate borough by Royal Charter. In 1554, soon after Mary was established on the throne, Banbury received a Charter of Incorporation from her. It appears from the preamble that this was granted as a reward to the inhabitants for their support of the Queen's cause when the Duke of Northumberland attempted to place Lady Jane Grey on the throne. Under this charter, Banbury's Corporation or council was to consist of a bailiff, 12 aldermen and 12 burgesses. The first bailiff was William Barnsley and his successors were to be elected each year from amongst the aldermen. This council had the power to create what amounted to bylaws that ensured a more satisfactory government of the town. In line with a centuries

23 *Parsons Street was central to prebendal land.*

old tradition, Banbury was granted a weekly market along with two fairs on feast days 1 August (Lammas Day) and 18 October (St Luke's). To ensure that there were no problems during the fairs a Court of Piepowder was created for the specific purpose of dealing with these as they arose and with actions arising from the market such as the collection of rents and taxes, the stallage and piccage levies.[3]

The area governed by this charter was the old medieval town, so parts of the ecclesiastical parish in the surrounding hamlets and Grimsbury over the bridge in Northamptonshire were outside its boundaries. The urban area was very clearly demarcated by its bar gates and had a population of about 1,000 with a system of government based around the town hall located at that time in Cornhill. Here the corporation

adopted the motto *DOMINUS NOBIS SOL ET SCUTUM* (For the Lord is a sun and shield) and the sun symbol at the centre of this inscription can still be found on many extant buildings.

The charter also gave the bailiff, aldermen and burgesses of the borough and parish of Banbury the power to nominate and elect 'one discreet Burgess' to serve as M.P. for the borough. During the reigns of Elizabeth and the early Stuarts the Copes of Hanwell and Fiennes of Broughton provided most of Banbury's Members of Parliament and there were no disputed elections until the 1680s.

A dinner for the members of the Corporation was the occasion for celebrating the granting of the new charter. Brinkworth has suggested that this was a sumptuous affair with 'capons, conies, geese, bread, ale, wine and fruit, in the form of

24 *Foundations and cellars of ironstone buildings in Bridge Street – an important part of the post-medieval urban area.*

a hundred pears'. The townsfolk had their own event, a pageant in the Horse Fair.

A fine vision of Tudor Banbury is contained in Leland's account of the town dated between 1535 and 1543. His site descriptions make the essential distinction between low-lying meadow and marsh close to the River Cherwell and drier rising ground on the south and south-west perimeter. Central to his account is the Market Place with its cross and 'a purle of fresh water' – clearly the Cuttle Brook; nearby was the massive stone castle originally built on the orders of Bishop Alexander, that until 1646 doubled as a prison, whilst at the western end of the town was the impressive church founded in the 12th century.

Banbury's historians have spent much time and effort trying to establish the location of the cross made famous by the nursery rhyme. The Victorians decided it stood at the western end of the High Street and erected a commemorative cross, the present Banbury Cross, on the spot. The cross of Leland's account is most likely to have stood in Cornhill close to his 'fairest street', which Harvey has interpreted as Bridge Street. The earliest documentary evidence for this cross is a 1478 bequest by William Saunders intended to cover the cost of repairing the stone cross in front of his property on Barkhill Street, the then name for the northern fringe of the Market Place along with what is now Cornhill. This cross was the Market or High Cross and appears to have had three stone steps leading up to its cruciform shape.[4]

A second or Bread Cross has been traced to the junction of Butchers Row and the eastern end of Sheep Street, now High Street. It was recorded in the rental of 1441 and then acknowledged in a royal grant of 1549. In 1604 Matthew Knight, who was a local property owner, had a shop in the vicinity and was aware of the Bread Cross near to where butchers and bakers had stalls.

The White Cross stood on the junction of West Bar Street and what is now Beargarden Road. It marked the western boundary of the borough and, according to Harvey, found mention in two separate records. In 1554 there is a description of a 'White Cross outside the gate called Sugarforde Gate' (West Bar). A later reference of 1606 incorporates the significant but vague 'the great stone called the White Crosse'.

Banbury's crosses were destroyed at the outset of the 17th century, one outcome of an increasing Puritan zeal in the area. The action is reflected in a poem by Richard Corbet that has the following relevant lines: 'The Crosses also like old stumps of trees, or stools for horsemen that have feeble knees, carry no heads

25   *The second Town Hall located in the Market Place.*

26   *The medieval meadows of Banbury included the Cherwell Wetlands.*

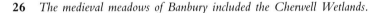

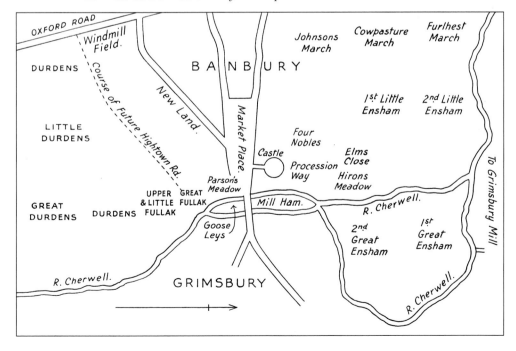

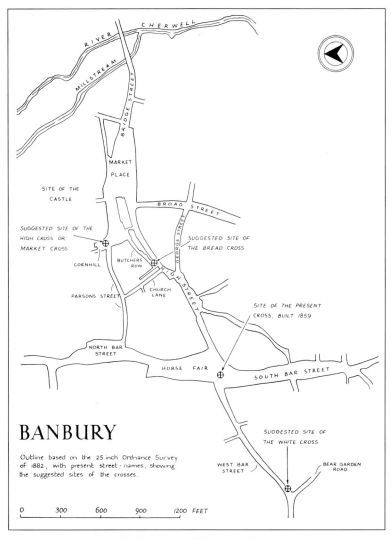

27   *The sites of Banbury Crosses.*

St John's Bar and the North Bar were at the town boundaries on the key north-south road, which would have been a *via principia* had Banbury enjoyed a Roman existence. The former gate had an arch about 12 feet wide. Sugarford Bar was where a narrow lane called the Shades crossed the western route into the medieval town – named the Bull Bar Street of 1653 after a nearby inn called the *Bull*. This bar had a main archway for the passage of anything on wheels and a subsidiary doorway for those on foot. It appears to have been rebuilt after a fire of 1628. The Cole Bar was on the way leading into the castle from the Oxford Road. It also underwent reconstruction in the 17th century. Bridge Bar was the least well known of the gates but had added significance because the way across the Cherwell was the divide between Oxfordshire and Northamptonshire.

When Leland focused on the buildings of the town he noted several characteristic architectural features. The *Red Lion* in the Beast Market (lower High Street) had a gateway whose columns were of Perpendicular style whereas the *White Horse* near the Sheep Street extension to the High Street was characterised by a doorway designed in 14th-century style. Even in the nearby Neithrop township there were a few notable features such as a house on the south side of Boxhedge Lane that had an early 15th-century window.

above ground …'.[5] Harvey quotes 1648 as the last date of documentary source material on the topic.[6] Over 200 years then elapsed before a prospective royal wedding in Queen Victoria's reign inspired Banburians to erect a new cross in 1859.[7]

In Leland's day there were five gates or bar entrances to the town – St John's, Sugarford, North, Cole and Bridge. Alfred Beesley suggests that they were erected not for defensive reasons but mainly because of a need to collect tolls.[8]

Banbury's streets were in a very poor state according to Leland. Even the principal ones were rutted and street cleaning varied greatly in frequency. Butchers Row received weekly attention but in 'Mylne Lane' (Mill Lane) quarterly action was considered adequate. However, precautions were taken to ensure that the Gooseleys near the river bridge were not polluted and that St Mary's churchyard was kept free of livestock excrement, and the Cuttle Brook was not allowed to attract harmful waste. Leland wrote that no man might 'suffere geyse or doukes to goo in the same brouke' nor 'sett any honey barrelles or other vessel in souke'.

Banbury was the most important market within a wide agricultural area. Someone whose activities illustrated this on a grand scale was Richard Walker from near Shipston-on-Stour. He was known to have had as many as 500 sheep in pens stretched out along the length of Sheep Street from Butchers Row to just short of where the 1859 cross was erected. However, Matthew Knight, a mercer, in a deposition to the Court of Star Chamber at the beginning of the 17th century, complained that the increasing puritanical zeal of the leading members of the Corporation was driving away the country gentlemen and people from the areas around the town and that they were using other market towns; his own trade had suffered badly. The account may well be biased as he was in dispute with William Knight and other members of the Corporation and would naturally want to paint as black a picture as possible.

Nationally the growth of the cloth trade had led to an expansion of pastureland for sheep at the expense of arable land. Banbury had long had an association with the wool and cloth trade and it is probable that the change of land use from arable to pasture in Neithrop was for sheep. The parish of Banbury had five separate field systems still in operation in the 16th century. At the beginning of the century little of this land was enclosed and in most cases holdings were scattered, but the trend was to consolidation and by the early 17th century much of the Calthorpe estate was enclosed and most probably converted to sheep pasture. In Hardwick the Cope family gradually turned the estate into an enclosed farm.

By Tudor times few people living inside the borough depended on the land for a living. Exceptions were seven husbandmen, five yeomen, a gardener and shepherd. Wills and inventories give a good idea of the nature and significance of trades.[9]

Trade	% of all Trades
Leatherworking	34
Suppliers of food and drink	26
Cloth trade	16
Wood working	9
Metal working	8
Building trades	3

There were 50 leatherworkers, which helps to explain the importance to Banbury of shoemaking before 1640. In the late 16th century the scale of operations suggested an output beyond even local needs. This is the evidence from 30 wills of Banbury shoemakers from the period 1551-1640 and six from 1640 to 1730. They suggest that as Banbury's importance declined that of Northampton increased. However wills are not a complete guide to the prosperity of this trade.

Included among the leatherworkers were skinners, fellmongers, white leather workers and tanners. A leading skinner in 1592 was Robert Poope, whose range of skins included a lining of black coney (rabbit fur) for a petticoat. Existing inventories indicate only one white leather worker, Robert Clemson, who was better known as a purse maker and glover. Amongst the other glovers, John Rylie had a good business in 1602. Twenty dozen gloves were worth £2 10s. 6d. Some of his gloves are recorded as being on sale at Bicester Fair, which was an August sheep fair.

28 *West Bar Street and Sugarford Bar in the 18th century.*

Banbury supported three peddlers, John Perein and his son Thomas and a Simon Harvey. Their inventories reveal a heavy involvement with horse-related equipment. Versatility rather than high quality appears to have been the hallmark of Banbury's craft products. Leather jacks and buckets were on offer as well as shoes, and amongst the latter were some 'unsaleable shoes' in the stock of Thomas Pedlie.

The clothing trades achieved prominence in Banbury from about 1225. They embraced a diversity of trades including weavers, clothworkers, tailors, mercers and woollen drapers. Many people in the first three of these categories were fairly poor, small master craftsmen, journeymen and artisans. The average inventory value for clothworkers was only just over £9, whereas the woollen draper Thomas Halhed had total goods valued at nearly £170. By 1600 a governing class of merchants and

industrialists supported by lawyers and other professional men was emerging. Woollen drapers and mercers were the chief merchants of Banbury and their weaving activities extended into the surrounding rural area.

The differences between town and country dwellers in Tudor England were not so marked as they became in the 19th century. Many houses and shops still had considerable plots of land attached to them. A number of traders, such as John Walker, a butcher, would have derived some of their income from farming. Some people living in Banbury cultivated land and pastured livestock on the town's common fields.

Considering Banbury's importance as a market town and trading centre it is perhaps surprising that those involved with the preparation and sale of food and drink were not always prosperous. Sixteenth-century Banbury

29   *The* Red Lion *in Banbury's Beast Market.*

had six bakers, four of whom had the means of delivering their own bread. Amongst the more successful of these was Edward Welchman, who first prepared Banbury Cakes at the famous Parsons Street shop.

The town was also renowned for its ale, even though brewing does not appear to have been on the industrial scale that developed later. Outlets for beer were numerous and in some cases of considerable note. John Knight, who built the *Reindeer Inn* in Parsons Street in 1570, was one of the foremost inhabitants of the town and Henry Wright, one of the richest, was the first known licensee of the *Three Swans* (now the *Swan*) in 1545. This inn in St John's Street (South Bar) appears to have been large enough to boast a number of rooms, such as the 'Willowbee', the 'Great Chamber' and several others with names. It also had three stables.

As in many market towns, specific traders used to be concentrated in particular parts of the urban area. Banbury had several streets and spaces dedicated to a trade or some form of market activity. While butchers occupied Butchers' Row, Sheep Street, Cow Fair and Haymarket were all reminders of the town's involvement with livestock.

Sheep Street had been the medieval town's Guler Street and in the early 17th century was sometimes referred to as Bolting or Breadcross Street. People who lived there used to rent out sheep pens, a valuable source of additional income even though the actual extent of the market may have fluctuated. In 1655 they were enraged by the Corporation's decision to move the sheep market and benefit from stallage. The exact location of the new site is unclear but references like 'remote from the houses' and 'dirty and mirlie land by reason of the

30   *The western end of Sheep Street (High Street) had the original sheep market.*

31   *The open fields in the Middle Ages.*

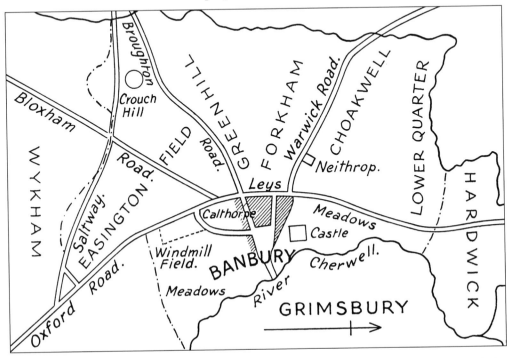

lowness of the ground' suggest somewhere towards the Cherwell or the Mill Stream rather than the western end of Leland's 'fair street'.

Many of the town's activities were unrelated to livestock. There were just four recorded mills, called Wykham, Grimsbury, Cuttle and Banbury. Repair work on them seems to have been in the hands of a single millwright called John Dryver. Woodworking incorporated several different trades, notably carpenter, carver, turner and wheelwright. The turner, who was Thomas Overburge (d.1606), had a shop in the Market Place which contained numerous digging tools as well as some spinning wheels.

Metalworkers were also a vital part of the community. There were six blacksmiths and their inventories included a wide range of tools of their trade. For instance, in 1643 William Avis, servant to Titus Buckingham, left possessions that included bellows and a sledgehammer as well a range of shoeing tools. Amongst the ironmongers in the town were the Hadleys, who were one of the leading families. Thomas, son of Humfrey, had a shop with a range of goods way beyond those you would expect to find today. His inventory included crossbows, lathes, anvils and tinder boxes. Items held by his brother Edward were even more varied and included Flanders kettles, old swords and various firearms.

32 *Ancient doorway of the* White Horse Inn *in the High Street.*

33 *Arriving at the* Reindeer *in Parsons Street.*

Four

PURITANS, CIVIL WAR AND RESTORATION 1603 TO 1700

On 15 September 1606 Banbury's borough boundary was determined in some detail. In the following November this formed the basis of a presentation by a jury consisting of the leading townsmen appointed by a Mr Hersye, the King's Surveyor. The boundary commenced from the eastern arch of the bridge over the Cherwell

34 *William Whateley, vicar of Banbury and a leading Puritan.*

and then followed the course of the river southwards, on the east side of a plot of land called Gooseleys, as far as and across Parsons Meadow and over a close of one Thomas Halhead. Beyond here the course was by way of Gattridge Close and Calthorpe Lane to the South Bar, also called St John's Bar. From here it followed the lane between various closes and Calthorpe Field (the Shades) to the White Cross stone, which stood at the western end of the present West Bar, just east of the junction with Bear Garden Road.

The next part of its route was across a stream at the north end of Barridge Leys (now the People's Park) and through a short lane by the house of one Edward Keeling. It then followed the course of another stream to the North Bar. Beyond this northern gate to the town the boundary coincided with the Cuttle Brook to the rear of the houses by the castle moat, then on to the Cuttle Mill and so to where the Cuttle Brook joined the Cherwell. The course of the river led back to the bridge's eastern arch. This boundary remained unchanged until the borough was extended in 1889.[1]

35 *Well-known political cartoon of the Puritan hanging his cat.*

Shortly after establishing the boundaries, the council petitioned James I for a new charter. Granted in June 1608, this extended the privileges of the Corporation, and made the borough a mayoral town, the chief officer now styled mayor instead of bailiff. The Common Council was to consist of 12 burgesses named as aldermen, from whom the mayor would be chosen, and six others designated chief burgesses. In addition 'there shall be within the Borough 30 honest and discreet men who shall be helpers or Assistants of the Borough'. Provision was also made for a Recorder and Chamberlain (treasurer). Vacancies were filled from the rank below, aldermen from the chief burgesses, chief

burgesses from the assistants, and new assistants from suitable 'honest and discreet men'. The members of the council were elected for life and some of the officers served for a very long period. Given the close relationship between many of them it was easy to exclude townspeople with opposing views from any part in the government of the town. The power to make bylaws was confirmed and the system of administering justice laid down. Important in the light of a later dispute was the procedure for electing a mayor should the mayor die before the end of his term of office or be deposed. The charter also required the provision of a prison or gaol within the borough, the mayor to be the keeper thereof.[2]

36 *A lone cart trundles towards Sheep Street.*

During the late 16th and into the early 17th centuries Banbury was greatly influenced by extreme and radical ways known as Puritanism. Its origins can be sought in the growth of Protestantism, which was particularly noticeable amongst the more prosperous merchants and tradesmen. Within the church an early exponent was Thomas Brasbridge, who was inducted at St Mary's in 1581. This nonconforming clergyman remained in post for nine years during which time he gathered around him a significant group of the town's leading inhabitants, who argued in favour of his being able to preach when he was deprived of the living in 1590. As it happens, his death in 1593 and the appointment of Ralph Houghton as his successor ensured much more conformity to the established church.

In 1610, twenty years after the Brasbridge incumbency, Banbury welcomed its most famous vicar, William Whateley, son of Thomas and Joyce Whateley and thus a member of one of Banbury's leading families. Thomas Whateley had had substantial involvement in local affairs as he had been a Justice of the Peace and also twice mayor of the borough. During his time at Cambridge University William Whateley became a disciple of Dr Chaderton Perkins, who was a leading Puritan of the day.

Whateley was vicar of Banbury for 30 turbulent years and was a popular figurehead. Because of his voice and style of preaching he became known as 'the Roaring Boy of Banbury'. Sir Edward Leigh, a well-read contemporary, commented, 'Oh, with what life and zeale would hee both preach and pray! How strict and watchful was hee in his whole life.'[3] Whateley was remembered for many sermons, perhaps the best known being 'Sinne No More', which was about the terrible fire of 1628. Ironically the first alarm was given whilst Whateley was administering the holy sacrament. This led him to comment that 'the fire came riding as it were in triumph through your streetes ... till it had passed from end to end of your towne, and could not be restrained'. He linked the event to what he called 'God's displeasure for our sinners' and added that Banbury people should not mock Puritanism. The whole sermon occupied two hours. When it came to Holy Communion he insisted on people sitting rather than kneeling – very much a Puritan practice. Whateley died in 1639 and was not only buried in the churchyard but was considered worthy of a monument to his memory.

The fire itself is said to have started in a West Bar Street malthouse during the Sunday morning of 2 March 1628.

> Within the space of foure houres that fire was carried from one end of the Towne to the other with that fury ... it consumed 103 dwelling houses, 20 kilne-houses and other out-houses ... Together with so much malt and other graine and commodities as amounted at the least to the value of twenty thousand pounds.[4]

The impact of the fire on the topography of Banbury can only be inferred from the appearance of the town at a later date when new buildings had replaced earlier timber and plaster structures. Existing histories of Banbury are broadly in agreement that the fire engulfed West Bar, South Bar, Calthorpe Lane, Fish Street and Colebar Street. The process of rejuvenation seems to have involved re-orientation of some roads, notably Calthorpe Lane and Colebar Street. The latter appears to have been shifted westwards.

There can be little doubt also that the fire caused great distress. William Whateley appealed for financial help and it is interesting to note that Coventry contributed just over £26, sufficient to help 65 people. Another aspect of the post-fire trauma was the likelihood of civil disorder. With this in mind, soldiers appear to have been drafted in to keep the peace, an action that according to Beesley carried the risk of

further physical damage in the parts of the town that had escaped the fire.

One significant piece of rebuilding was the re-erection of the West or Sugarford Bar in 1631. Appropriately, above the main arch a stone was inserted which carried the inscription, 'Except the Lord keep the city, the watchman watcheth but in vain'.

Another prominent Puritan of the day was Anthony Cope of Hanwell Castle, who was Banbury's Member of Parliament. Cope was a staunch opponent of the May Day festivities that had been part of the traditions of the town. He used his influence in a dispute over the erection of a maypole in 1589 and the suppression of Whitsun-ales, May Games and Morris Dances. John Danvers of Calthorpe Manor, who was also Sheriff of Oxford, was strongly opposed to these decisions but in the end was forced to accept the consequences of Cope's actions.

The maypole disappeared from the streets of Banbury in 1589 but this was only the start. In 1600 the Bread Cross and High Cross had been destroyed as objects of superstition. The Star Chamber suit, which referred to the destruction of the crosses, accused William Knight, the town's leading Puritan, and a small group of aldermen of inciting controversies. Small wonder Banbury was dubbed a place of 'cakes and zeale' and became a byword for extreme Puritanism.

Its reputation is well documented by contemporary writers in the first half of the 17th century. One of the best known allusions appears in *Barnabee's Journal*, written by Richard Braithwaite around 1616:

> In my progresse travelling Northward, Taking
> my farewell o'th' Southward,
> To Banbery came I, O prophane one!
> Where I saw a Puritane one
> Hanging of his cat on Monday
> For killing of a mouse on Sunday.

This entry was hugely popular and several editions appeared between 1716 and 1822. What varied was the method of hanging the cat in the accompanying illustrations: from a broom attached to a post, from a tree and from a hook on a shelf. This action was recognised as a satire against people of 'an extravagantly precise conscience'. The phrase 'Banbury man', first used by Ben Jonson in his play *Bartholomew Fair* in 1614, soon came to be used of any Puritan whether from Banbury or elsewhere.

Unsurprisingly, the effects of Puritanism combined with the catastrophic impact of the 1628 fire meant that morale in the town was at a very low ebb. It was especially unfortunate that an ongoing struggle between King and Parliament culminated in the Civil War between the Royalists and Parliamentarians which occupied the years between 1642 and 1649 and caused further damage and disruption.[5]

In 1634 opposition to the king's increasing use of the Prerogative of the Crown to raise the money needed for foreign wars became focused on Ship Money. Charles needed revenue to support his navy and Parliament was unwilling to pay, but his lawyers discovered that according to ancient laws the whole land should pay for the upkeep of the fleet. The difficulty was that for a long time only maritime counties had been asked to pay. In August 1635 Charles levied 'Ship Money' on the whole country, leading to widespread protests. The county of Oxford was reckoned on the basis of one ship of 280 tons and 112 men. In money terms this was £3,500. Banbury's share was £40, payment of which was made difficult by the effects of the great fire. Francis Andrew, mayor of Banbury, endeavoured to get part of this amount remitted but without success and in the end his efforts cost the Corporation the sum of £1 6s. 8d. for his journey to London.

A series of letters written in the summer of 1637 by Nathaniel Wheatly, mayor, to William Walter, Sheriff of Oxford, explained the impossible position Wheatly found himself in. Although the appropriate warrants were issued, the constables and other officers absolutely refused to collect the money. He had tried to get in the sum levied himself but many shut their doors against him and threatened to sue if their goods were taken in lieu of the tax. The king ordered that Wheatly should receive protection and any cases against him be removed to Westminster. The three constables were taken before the Council in London and briefly imprisoned. They were released after promising never to offend again and entering into a bond to collect the arrears of ship money.

By the 1640s the leading Puritan in the area and an important figure nationally was Viscount Seye and Sale of Broughton Castle, holder of Banbury Castle and High Steward of the Borough. In 1642, with events moving closer to an armed struggle, Parliament gave him charge of the Oxfordshire Militia. Nor was this the full extent of the family's influence on local affairs. His eldest son, James, sat as member for Oxfordshire, and his second son, the Hon. Nathaniel Fiennes, as member for Banbury.

The first armed encounter took place at the end of July when a party of men led by Lord Brook, who was escorting some pieces of ordnance from Banbury to Warwick Castle, was intercepted by a Royalist force led by the Earl of Northampton. After much debate it was agreed to move the ordnance back to Banbury. This led to the town being fortified and guns placed on Crouch Hill. On 7 August the town was attacked by a party of 500 to 600 Royalist horse, which threatened to fire the town if the ordnance were not delivered up. The unfortunate Mr Wheatly was sent to parley with them and the ordnance was surrendered and taken to Compton Wynyates, home of the Royalist leader, the Earl of Northampton.

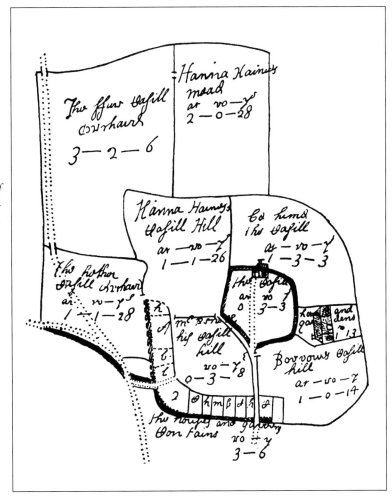

37 Lord Saye and Sele of Broughton Castle was the 17th-century owner of Banbury Castle. This is the plan of its layout.

Although Edge Hill and Cropredy Bridge were massive confrontations in the Banbury area, and there were numerous minor skirmishes, the impact on Banbury itself was surpassed by the two sieges of the castle that was the ultimate cause of its destruction and resulted in depopulation of the urban area. The first and great siege began on Sunday 25 August 1644. At dawn on that day two companies of Parliamentary foot soldiers moved into the town and took control of St Mary's Church and yard. From here they began the process of knocking on doors searching for those Cavaliers who might be in houses near the castle.

An hour after daybreak Cavalier forces emerged from the castle with about 100 musketeers and horse support. From nearby gardens and houses they shot at the Roundhead forces and succeeded in making them retreat to the Town's End. Then the Parliamentary forces forced the Royalist soldiers into the streets and ultimately back inside the castle, a wall of which was pierced during the assault by canons placed in St Mary's churchyard.

Three days later the assault on the castle and its royal garrison was well under way. The besiegers and the besieged kept up a ceaseless cannonade. The arrival of Cromwell's Colonel

John Fiennes, the third son of Lord Saye and
Sele of Broughton, should have been a signal to
those inside that they ought to surrender. Sir
William Compton, son of the Earl of
Northampton and castle commander, gave an
unequivocal response – so long as one man was
left alive he was prepared to stand firm, an
attitude that could be interpreted as either folly
or genuine bravery. What is certain is that at
the end of August 1644 the force hostile to the
king was estimated at 3,500 horse and foot
together with a garrison of 400 troops.

At the start of September came the big push
for the castle. Parliamentary cannon were located
at the bottom of North Bar and close to the Bar
itself. In mid-17th-century Banbury this part of
the town comprised open meadowland and
nothing stood between the entrenched attackers
and the west wall of the castle. But a factor
greatly underestimated at the time was the height
of the water table. A solution was sought in the
use of Warwickshire miners from the Bedworth
area. Despite their specialist knowledge they
were defeated by an increasing quantity of water
and there seemed to be no real alternative to
the incessant cannonading that culminated in
the siege incident of 23 September. As the
miners had drained the outer moat it was
necessary to use quantities of furze to traverse
the muddy surface. The target point was a breach
in the castle's western wall, but such a limited
point of access carried the accelerated risk of
being repulsed and so it proved, death and injury
within the Parliamentary forces leading to
withdrawal and failure of the mission.

King Charles realised there was a desperate
need for support at Banbury and his response
was to dispatch the Earl of Northampton and
Colonel Gage. The two met at Adderbury but
between them and the castle stood some 800
mounted Parliamentarians strategically located
on open ground where suburban Easington
sprawls today. The Roundhead troops were put

to flight and the castle was at last relieved.

By the late autumn of 1644 distress due to
the incessant bombardment was replaced by the
effects of a plague that decimated the town.
This was most probably a virulent form of
typhoid fever. Sequences of burials entered in
the Banbury register were often prefaced by
statements like 'these supposed to dye of the
plague in this month of Aprill'. The disease
showed no respect for age or status. The list for
April includes a tailor and two butchers and a
number of soldiers, especially those who had
been part of the garrison in the castle. Many of
the inhabitants of the town were described as
'being recalled by name only in the memory of
whom the mourners go about the streets'.
Perhaps it was just as well that 1645 was relatively
peaceful. Somewhat ironically, it was on the
anniversary of the Guy Fawkes plot that King
Charles enjoyed a meal at the castle that had
successfully withstood the impact of civil
conflict. He was on his way back to Oxford.

This was not the end of the castle's
involvement in the war but the so-called 'second
episode' was a more subdued affair. It began on
23 January 1646 when Colonel Whalley
advanced on Banbury with troops assembled in
Northamptonshire and Warwickshire. Their
numbers exceeded 1,000 when the castle
garrison was a mere 300. But Whalley's men
were short of artillery and it was not until the
position of King Charles became untenable, in
late April 1646, that the castle garrison led by
Sir William Compton surrendered under very
favourable terms.

In the aftermath of these sieges, Lord Saye
and Sele of Broughton was compensated for the
castle, which by then belonged to him. With
the end of the war the inhabitants of Banbury
were successful in getting Parliament to agree
to the demolition of what remained of the
structure and townspeople were allowed to use
the materials for the repair of their own

38   *Robins Bros. building sustained Civil War musket ball damage.*

properties, many of which had suffered musket ball damage. A typical example was the building on the corner of the Market Place and Butchers Row that was to become the Robins family ironmongers shop in the late 19th century.

A notable characteristic of the post-Civil War town was depopulation. The St Mary's parish register records just 26 burials in 1647 and 30 in 1648. The effects of the conflict were also felt in the surrounding countryside, where productivity was much reduced in a landscape that Camden had observed was rich and fertile.

Oliver Cromwell had to deal with a number of insurrections organised by a dissident groups, the strongest of whom, known as the Levellers, condemned the new Council of State describing it as 'a factious Juncto and Councel of State, usurping and assuming the name, stamp, and authority of Parliament, to oppress, torment, and vex the People'. Locally their leader was a Captain William Thompson, who had been a

corporal in Colonel Whalley's regiment at the siege of Banbury in 1646. In May 1649 he was in the Banbury area, where his supporters were thought to number about 200. Their downfall came on 10 May when, as Colonel Reynolds reports, 'It hath pleased God to bring this great Bubble of the Levellers about Banbury to a sudden breaking'. In an encounter near Warkworth the rebels yielded to Colonel Reynolds. The rank and file were dismissed but the officers detained. Thompson himself escaped and fled through Banbury towards Chipping Norton and met up with a body of Levellers numbering about 5,000 at Burford. Cromwell himself and Colonel Reynolds mounted a surprise night attacked that ended the Levellers' insurrection. Thompson escaped once again but was pursued and finally shot in a wood near Wellingborough.

In July 1653 a survey was taken of the property in Banbury of 'Charles Stuart late King

39 *A Civil War trial scene at the* Reindeer's Globe Room *in Parsons Street.*

of England'. This gives further topographical information, listing properties by street, detailing rooms and tenants' names, and in some cases providing an indication of damage suffered in the Civil War: 'North Bar Street: A piece of ground whereon two tenements lately stood, but destroyed by fire in the late war, in the occupation of John Owen'. We also get fresh insight into property values in the centre of the town. Three tenements or cottages in the possession of William Boodle located in Sheep Street were said to have a rent value of £5. In the Beast Market a tenement of Elizabeth Glover was valued at £3 10s. and one whose occupant was a man called Plampton fetched £5. This same street also had several plots left vacant as a result of the 1628 fire.

Four years after this survey, members of Banbury's Corporation were involved in a Chancery lawsuit that had considerable implications for the status of a street and its property. The issue was an attempt to remove the weekly sheep market from Sheep Street, part of Banbury's High Street in Tudor and Stuart times. Jeremy Gibson in an article for *Cake and Cockhorse* stressed that house owners here used to set out pens in front of their properties on market days and received rents from these, which improved their quality of life and tenement values. It appears they had a right to do this under a Corporation bylaw of 1564, and residents of Sheep Street such as William Weston were prepared to defend this right if necessary. Gibson suggests that, although the stallholders were at first successful in preventing immediate loss of the facility, the outcome of the lawsuit is not known and the probability must be that the Corporation was ultimately successful in securing a change of location to a part of the Horse Fair.[6]

In post-Restoration Banbury it was the turn of some nonconformist sects to feel the full weight of the law. Quakers especially were misunderstood when they refused to take an

40 *The house of Edward Vivers, Quaker cloth merchant.*

oath of allegiance to the king (they did not swear oaths of any kind). This was interpreted as disloyalty and often resulted in legal proceedings. The cloth merchant Edward Vivers, whose house still stands in the High Street, found himself committed to Oxford gaol. In spite of this the Quakers were able to establish a meeting house in Banbury, the second of which was built in 1664 on the site of the present meeting house in the north-west corner of the Horse Fair. On a wider front, the vicar of Banbury at the time of the Restoration, Samuel Wells, lost the living in 1662 for refusal to conform and was forced to move to Deddington in 1665 under the Five Mile Act though he kept in touch with his former parishioners.

Although the charters acquired during the reigns of Mary and James I in common with many other boroughs were surrendered to the crown to avoid the forfeiture many feared, the acquisition of a new charter in 1683 brought an enlargement of the jurisdiction of the Justices to include the hamlets of Calthorpe, Easington, Wykham, Neithrop and Hardwick, or all the parish of Banbury that was in Oxfordshire. But the real purpose of the new charter came in a proviso that gave the king and his heirs the power to dismiss any mayor, members of the Corporation, or its officers if he so wished. In this way the crown hoped to influence the selection of a Member of Parliament who would be favourable to its policies. Ironically, the loss of the earlier charters was only temporary because the surrender process was never formalised. Under a proclamation of James II in 1688, which was read in the open market and affixed to one of the posts on the Market House, the charters were restored and the members of the Corporation who had been ejected by Charles regained office.

Though most people must have looked favourably on this royal decision it did not save James' throne. There was mounting opposition

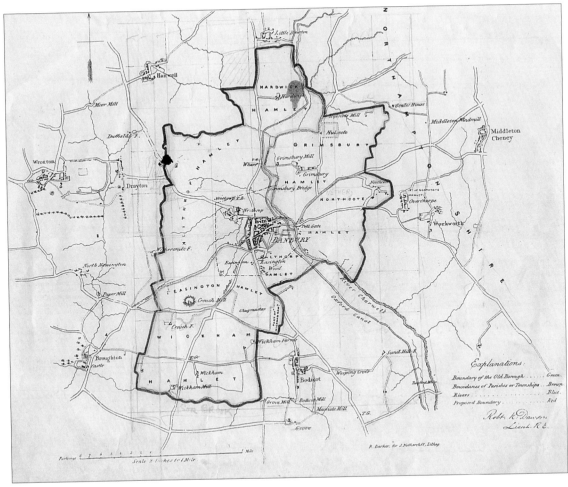

41   *The enlarged Banbury of 1683.*

both locally and nationally to royal interference in local government, which culminated in the king's forced abdication in December 1688. The following January a new Parliament was called by William of Orange and Sir Robert Dashwood of Wykham, who was Banbury's representative, was amongst those who offered the crown to the Prince of Orange and his wife Princess Mary, daughter of James II.

The old charters were again forfeited in 1717, when two groups representing the Hanoverians and Jacobites could not agree on the election of a mayor, so that when the mayor's term of office came to an end there was no one to succeed him. The charter automatically lapsed and, with it, the Corporation's right to govern the town. The town had to petition George I for a new charter, which was duly granted on 16 July 1718. Its terms were very similar to the one it replaced with the important provision that the mayor would continue in office until a successor was elected.

Five

THE ROAD TO RECOVERY
1700 TO 1800

The dawn of the 18th century was a time to reflect on the consequences of Civil War and Puritan outrage. The town was governed according to the charter of 1718 so the people of the town had no say in who controlled their affairs. The Corporation was not responsible for health matters or the state of the roads and its members presided over a town that had no proper drainage or street lighting. In these pre-police days watchmen were the people concerned with public safety.

The members of the Corporation appear to have constituted a somewhat exclusive and self-perpetuating club made up of the more reactionary local people who foregathered to eat and drink and occasionally elect a Member of Parliament. Banbury was one of only five constituencies that returned a single Member of Parliament. The connection of the North family with the borough began in 1672 when the 1st Lord Guilford acquired a perpetual lease on the house and estate at Wroxton from Trinity College, Oxford, on his marriage to Lady Frances Pope, heiress daughter of the last Earl of Downe. For most of the 18th century and up to the Great Reform Act, Banbury was the family's pocket borough. The earlier Norths were strong Tories but by 1727, when the Hon. Francis North became M.P., he was standing as a Whig.

That the Corporation could have a mind of its own was demonstrated two years later when Francis North succeeded his father as Lord Guilford. His nominee, Lord Wallingford, was unexpectedly defeated by one vote, a result that Lord Guilford felt was caused by Lord Wallingford's not taking the trouble to canvass for the votes of the Corporation. In 1733 Lord Wallingford was again the candidate and this time great care was taken to 're-establish the friendship which used to subsist between my family [the Norths] and the corporation'. Wallingford was elected unopposed and continued to represent the borough until his death in 1740.

It was Lord Guilford's son, Fredrick Lord North, who really established the family hold on the Banbury constituency. Between 1754 (when he was aged 22) and 1790, Fredrick was elected 13 times. During this time his power was increased considerably by being appointed First Lord of the Treasury and then Prime Minister, 'the Prime Minister who lost America', for 12 years. The Norths played a significant role in the decisions taken by the Banbury Corporation and provided the opportunity of government patronage for several local people. Their contributions to the town included the 1711 rebuilding of the almshouses near St Mary's Church, to which they donated a bell in 1820. Their involvement in the endowment of the Blue Coat School was of paramount importance as was the administration of the Sprigge Charity.

Despite the rise of industries such as brewing and weaving, the Banbury area of the 18th century was largely agricultural and dependent upon related activities. Prior to the enclosure acts in the second half of the century the land was farmed much as it had been for centuries. Changes such as the introduction of the four-fold crop rotation, improvement in stock breeding and the development of the seed drill and horse hoeing had encouraged a movement towards enclosure by some of the more forward-looking aristocratic estates in some areas. Large open fields surrounded the town where strip cultivation still persisted. In 1688 these fields were called Hardwick, Neithrop, Calthorpe and Wykham. The fields of Neithrop and Wykham were subdivided into quarters. Neithrop consisted of Choakwell and Lower Quarter on the north side of the Warwick Road and Forkham and Greenhill Quarters on the other side.

Even with the open field system the profits from farming could be great. The government actively encouraged arable farming and the demand for wool was still high, which stimulated the move towards enclosure. Potts has shown that the large open field of Neithrop, 1,398 acres in size, was enclosed by an Act of Parliament of 1758. Two years later the Commissioners' Award brought together the open allotments into concentrated enclosed farms. The award that formalised their actions appears to have been put together at the *Three Tuns* in the Horse Fair. Within these enclosed farms sheep assumed a greater importance, a move driven by the need to provide meat as well as wool for growing urban settlements. A slightly later award drawn up in 1765 related to the enclosure of the open fields of Warkworth, which at that time included Grimsbury.[1]

By the beginning of the 19th century it was clear that the more intensive agricultural system was producing a new breed of farmers who were more knowledgeable than their predecessors and this showed during dealings at the Banbury markets.

Not everyone shared in their prosperity and the numbers claiming relief grew steadily after the enclosures of common land. The relief of the many poor people of the town was not the concern of the Corporation. Under the Poor Law dating from the reign of Elizabeth, which with minor modifications was still in force, the parish was responsible for relief. Since the 17th century Banbury had been divided into six or seven poor wards each with an overseer in charge. In turn this person was responsible to the Parish Vestry, although there were contributions in the form of charitable bequests. Occasional gifts became a significant source of help for some of the poor during the 18th century. Lord Guilford gave 10 guineas to Edward Box, mayor of Banbury, in 1773 for the benefit of the poor people at Christmas. In the same year he provided just short of £79 for poor families ravaged by outbreaks of smallpox.

Deaths from Smallpox	
1717	62
1718	124
1719	113
…	…
1731	14
1733	80
…	…
1760	163

Someone else anxious to help victims of this disease was James West. His donation of £20 went towards the provision of money for nurses and the costs of burying the dead.

An important feature of concern for the poor of the town was the provision of workhouse accommodation. There had been a workhouse in Scalding Lane (now George Street) since the 1640s though it was not until an Act of George I in 1723 that the creation of workhouses was encouraged. Joshua Sprigge, a Banbury-born Puritan writer, bequeathed £500 to the Corporation of Banbury for the construction of a workhouse so that the poor of the area had the opportunity of work. A little over £440 from Sprigge's bequest was used to erect a new building that opened in 1731 on the east side of South Bar. The balance of the money, added to other financial resources, enabled the purchase of land for a further workhouse in Gould's Square in Neithrop. The interest on the fund was paid to the Chamberlain of the Corporation, who then repaid £26 a year to the poor rate and £4 to a baker who provided 20 loaves every first Sunday of the month. By mid-century a figure of about 1s. 2d. per person was being allocated for feeding, lodging and clothing. However, not all governors did a good job of administering this and in 1765 John Grant was found guilty of supplying unwholesome food to the inmates.

By the end of the 18th century, coping with an ever-increasing number of poor in workhouses was overwhelming the system. In an effort to combat this, the parish officers who were responsible for administering relief were authorised to use money from the poor rate to supplement wages and avoid sending more people to the overburdened workhouses. Although this helped the working classes in the short term, it benefited the employers even more as it enabled them to reduce wages, thus forcing the parish ratepayers to contribute to the wage bill through the poor rate.

42   *A typical stage coach arrival at the* Red Lion, Banbury.

43   *Coach travelling could be a cold experience.*

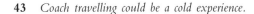

During the 18th century Banbury flourished as a market town partly because it was well served by a new development of turnpike roads, which led to Shipston-on-Stour, Southam, Chipping Norton, Lutterworth and Brackley. Each road had Turnpike Trustees who were empowered to raise money from tollgate receipts in return for the repair of road surfaces and bridges. The evolution of the turnpike routes was piecemeal, and in some places the Trustees were more interested in the fees than the repairs. However, gradual improvements in road engineering and the need for better and faster communications helped increase the efficiency of the stage-coaches. By 1750 a 30-hour journey from Banbury to London had been reduced to eight hours for mail coaches.

Before the arrival of canals in the latter half of the century, coaches dominated the transport scene. The first recorded example is the *Birmingham Stage Coach*, which commenced running on 24 May 1731. It operated between the West Midlands and London and passed through Banbury. Other early coaches were recorded in the *Oxford Journal*. Commencing in 1760, the *Banbury Machine* ran from the *Three Tuns* in the Horse Fair to London at a cost to the passenger of 10s. or 16s. Thirteen years later a different 'Machine' linked London's Holborn with the *Red Lion* in Banbury. The cost was only 8s. if you were prepared to travel outside. By 1792, Drinkwater's coach was operating between Oxford and the *Catherine Wheel* in Bridge Street.

Goods movement also benefited from the road improvements and facilitated the growth of the carriers' businesses. At the beginning of the century the state of the roads had meant packhorses were the only method of moving goods over any distance; by the second half of the century horse-drawn carts became a familiar sight on all the routes leading to Banbury. With very few exceptions, these carriers were men who made regular visits to the market town and provided a vital link for the village people without other forms of transport. Long distance journeys were covered by John Arne's wagons, which linked Oxford with Birmingham via Banbury, or Judd's Banbury Wagons.

By the end of the century, according to *Rusher's Lists* of 1798 and 1799, William Judd

was the only local wagoner with services to London and Birmingham. From 1797 he was a member of the Corporation and in 1799, 1805 and 1812 he wore the mayoral chain. Thirty-eight other carriers operated along shorter, more regional routes. They were typified by Mitchell of Warmington, who came to the *Plow* in Cornhill, and by Coleman from Adderbury, who was based at the *Kings Arms* in Parsons Street. Both men restricted their visits to Thursday (market day).

Some carriers served more than one village. Lock originated at Middleton Cheney but also called at Chacombe on his way to the *Catherine Wheel* in Bridge Street every Monday and Thursday. One man called Jessop reversed the procedure and went from his house in Banbury's Cow Fair to Thorpe and Culworth on Mondays and Fridays. Thursday, because it was Market Day, was when the greatest number of carriers appeared in the town.[2]

Rusher's List for 1798 seems to hint at very early examples of transport integration. Daniel Jabson ran to the wharf on the Oxford Canal from Shutford and North Newington, whilst Law of Thenford and Middleton had a wagon that connected with Judd's services. Another characteristic of the local carrier network was the relation to specific Banbury tradesmen. Plester of Kings Sutton terminated at Watson's shoemaking establishment on his Thursday runs.

Overall, the carriers who came to Banbury visited a total of 15 inns, half of which attracted more than one man. Seven of these premises were in the High Street and Parsons Street and only one, *The New Inn*, was in the hamlet of Neithrop.

The new roads were a factor in the changing nature of the urban inns of Banbury. Professor Alan Everitt has shown that Market Places were common locations for inns prior to the coaching era, when the 'chief requirement was a long site with a space to build extra chambers and

44   *A busy Cow Fair scene with many carriers' carts.*

warehouses and a back entrance so that wagons and coaches could enter the yard and leave it without turning and backing – an awkward problem for a horse-drawn vehicle'. The emergence of important inns in the 18th century was especially notable in 'thoroughfare towns' like Banbury.[3] A location on the principal road routes was crucial. The *Three Tuns* had plenty of space on the Horse Fair, that was also part of the main Oxford to Coventry and Oxford to Warwick roads.

Despite improvements the roads were an expensive way of carrying heavy and bulky goods over long distances. In coastal areas and on the major rivers water-borne trade had long been the preferred method of transport. Significant discussions about the need for an Oxford Canal took place in April 1768, when Sir Roger Newdigate of Arbury Hall near

Coventry, and owner of several coalmines, met various Banbury notables including Samuel Clarson who was mayor. The Warwickshire pit owner clearly felt the enterprise would result in a vital transport artery for his coal, and access to cheap coal was a major attraction for places along the canal.

By October 1768 plans for the proposed canal were ready for approval and a further meeting was held at the *Three Tuns*. The plans were formalised and parliamentary agreement and royal assent were secured by an Act of Authorisation dated 1768-9. The *Three Tuns* became the acknowledged location for company meetings. At the first of these James Brindley was appointed engineer and general surveyor. He came to the project with substantial experience gained working for the Duke of Bridgewater in north-west England.

Jackson's Oxford Journal for 1 October 1777 announced the opening of a wharf at Cropredy a few miles north of Banbury where coal was available at 5d. per cwt. On 30 March 1778 the canal link from Coventry to Banbury was completed and an initial load of 200 tons of coal reached the town at the same price as Cropredy, or 4½d. to those people carrying the fuel by wagon to any place over 14 miles from Banbury. In his *History of Banbury* William Potts records that the first coal to reach a local wharf was received 'amidst the loudest acclamations of a prodigious number of spectators', but local customers had to wait until mid-summer for 'the best Griff coals belonging to Sir Roger Newdigate to be sold at the wharf'.

---

4   RUSHER'S BANBURY LIST, 1798.

8. October 29th, being Old St. Luke's-Day.
9. December 13th, being the Second Thursday before Christmas.

In the Parish of Banbury, from Michaelmas 1796, to Michaelmas 1797, are registered,

113 Baptisms.
104 Burials.
34 Marriages.

N. B. The Burials of the Dissenters are included in this List, but not the Baptisms.

Officers of Neithrop, are,

Mr. Wm. Judge, Mr. W. Pratt, Mr. J. Roberts, Overseers
Wm. Eagles, High-Constable.
J. Salmon, Constable.
T. Cobb and H. Bolton, Surveyors.

The Excise Office, at the Buck and Bell.
The Stamp-Office, at Mr. W. Rusher's.
The Post comes in every Morning, about 10 o'Clock. Post Master, Mr. James King. Deputy Post Master, Mr. Joseph Wyatt, at the White Lion.
The Post-Office (at the White Lion) shuts every Day at 4 o'Clock.
The Mail Coach sets off every Day, from the White Lion, at Half past 4; passing through Woodstock and Oxford to the Bull and Mouth, London.
The Old Banbury Coach sets off from the Red Lion, every Sunday, Wednesday, and Friday, at 4 o'Clock, to the Bell and Crown, Holborn; and returns from thence

45   *An extract from* Rusher's List *for 1798.*

During the years between 1778 and 1790, when the canal finally reached Oxford, the terminus may well have been the main company wharf at Mill Lane known as the Old Wharf. This was adjacent to a basin big enough for canal boats to turn round. A further wharf was built in 1792 by James Golby, a grocer and coal merchant in Banbury. During this 12-year period Tooley's boatyard came into existence. Barry Trinder and Steve Litherland in their survey of the canal note that 'the smithy and dry-dock at Tooley's were both built in neat red clamped brick in the late 18th century'.[4]

Early commercial traffic on this narrow canal also included commodities like roadstone, lime and cement. Banbury and north Oxfordshire were on the eve of a communications revolution that was to place the town firmly on the country's map.

One of several buildings that suffered because of military action during the Civil War was the 12th-century St Mary's Church, whose fabric was in a bad state of disrepair by 1700. The Puritans responsible for dismantling the town's crosses had targeted internal treasures. Less easy to quantify but no less important a factor was neglect by townspeople. Some assistance with its repair came in the form of a £400 donation by Dr Fell, Bishop of Oxford, and timber was available from the last of the castles. But by just after the mid-century point the issue of St Mary's condition was again a matter of public concern. In 1772 it was decided to seek the advice of London surveyors who reported that the chancel, transepts and the tower were 'fit to stand for ages' but west of the tower the state of the church was deemed dangerous and rebuilding necessary.

No immediate action was taken and in 1784 it was again thought necessary to seek professional advice. Eighteen persons signed a resolution to the contrary but their protestations were ignored and a surveyor called Dalton was consulted. He advised the rebuilding of the north-west pillar close to the tower and the filling in of the arches on the south side. Potts doubted that work was ever done and pointed to a contrary report of 1784 in which it was categorically stated that St Mary's was as safe as St Paul's in London.

Five years later the same surveyor, in association with a buildings expert called Burton, highlighted the need for repairs costing about £2,100. The critical areas identified were the south aisle roof and the clerestory of the nave. Lowering the tower to the level of the roof was suggested, as well as the erection of a new tower at the west end.

By now the Vestry committee was beginning to have doubts about the future of the church. Its members called upon the professional services of the architect who had been responsible for the rebuilding of the cathedral church at Hereford. His advice was against restoration and on 17 March 1790 a bill was presented to the House of Commons for the demolition and rebuilding of the church. Even at such a late stage there were people opposed to this course of action and a formal written protest was signed by William Shirley, Samuel Grimbley and William Saunders but their opposition did not alter the course of events and in April 1790 Parliament gave the go-ahead for demolition.

The task of taking down the noble edifice was not without difficulties. Some parts had to be blown up with gunpowder and the great west window presented a particular challenge, despite the efforts of a team of 10 horses. When the work was finally completed some Banburians were left to reflect on the loss of a priceless memorial. The realisation that in the post-Civil War rebuilding of the town the church had not received the attention it merited had come too late.

The building of the new St Mary's was begun the same year and to the design of Robert Cockerill. His vision was for a church capable of holding 2,300 people and constructed of the local Horton stone. Much of this was extracted from a quarry near Broughton. Consecration of the new building was carried out on 6 September 1797 but completion of the building in its entirety was a project for the 19th century.[5]

An important religious issue in 18th-century Banbury was the revival of nonconformism. The Independents or Congregationalists started to meet during 1787 at the *Star Inn* in London Yard off Parsons Street and built a chapel in Church Passage five years later. In 1791 the first Wesleyan Society occupied a building in the passageway of Lodging House Yard that led from Calthorpe Street to South Bar. They may have been encouraged by a private visit to the town of John Wesley a year earlier.

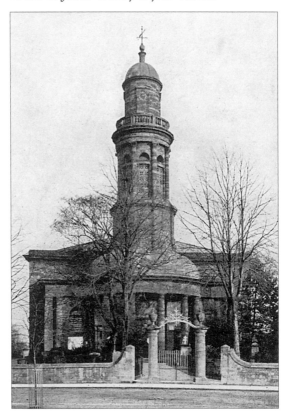

46 *The new St Mary's Church was consecrated in 1797.*

47   *Tar boats at Banbury.*

An outstanding educational development of the century was the founding of the Blue Coat Charity School in rooms above the borough gaol in the Market Place. An early task of the subscribers to the charity was to appoint a master and mistress to be responsible for the boys and girls respectively. A reflection of the different perception of the education for boys and girls is the amount of salary paid per year: £25 for the master and half that sum for the mistress. The former had to be an Anglican communicant and someone 'of sober life and conversation' who possessed 'a meek temper' and displayed 'humble behaviour'. His responsibilities included bringing the children to church on Sundays and the holy days of Christmas, Easter and Whitsun, and on weekdays whenever prayers were said. As for the mistress, she had to be of the same upbringing and was required to teach the girls to knit, sew, mark and spin.[6]

Banbury had its notable personalities. Two of these were John Cheney and William Rusher. The former was born at Great Rollright and first came to notice as the landlord of the *Unicorn Inn* where, according to the *New Daily Journal*, he had been installed in 1765. He was perhaps better known as a printer, and early account books suggest that he entered this occupation two years later. By 1771 he was busily engaged on a wide range of items that embraced summonses, warrants, sales catalogues, turnpike tickets, ballads, hymns and posters.

In 1788 Cheney left the *Unicorn* and took a shop in Red Lion Street where he established himself as a printer, bookseller and stationer. This proved to be a good decision and he prospered to the extent of supplying newspapers to the gentry. His proud boast was that the printing of items was effected in the neatest manner within the shortest period of notice and on the most reasonable terms. It is not surprising that his shop resembled a variety store, with cards, wood cuts, picture frames, sewing thimbles and garters. John died in 1808 but successors carried on the business, which continued with fluctuating success throughout the 19th century and beyond.

48 *A typical narrow boat on the Oxford Canal. Boat repair yard in background.*

49 *Oxford Canal south of Bridge Street, boundary of former Cherwell industrial area.*

50   *The lady on the White Horse, peace celebrations in 1919.*

William Rusher emerged from yeoman stock to be a bookseller in Banbury. In 1795 he started a remarkable series of Lists and Directories that were one day to become an important source of information about people, occupations and activities. His first issue was a single sheet which gave notice of the town authorities together with the names of the officers for the hamlet of Neithrop. It was given free to all those people who made purchases of an almanac or pocket book for 1796, possibly in response to an advertisement in *Jackson's Oxford Journal* for 6 December 1794.

When, at the age of 24, Will married Mary Golby in the old St Mary's Church on 9 February 1783, both were said to be of the parish. He was registered as a schoolmaster in the Banbury Bluecoat School by whom he was paid a salary of £24 5s. 6d. a year. This level of remuneration was not enough to cause him to give up his bookselling activities, and in 1792 William Arne, son of a local carrier, appears to have taken over the reigns of instruction at the charity school. Rusher had other sources of income notably in the form of rents from property in Neithrop and due to his shop acting as a stamp office in Banbury.

Rusher was truly a man of his town: parish clerk from 1795 to 1813, an overseer for the poor in 1797, and a churchwarden at St Mary's from 1806 to 1816. The last of these roles suggests the status gained by the income brought in from the sale of books, magazines and stationery.[7]

Even in the 18th century Banbury was widely known because of the 'Ride a cock-horse' rhyme.[8] An early version first appeared in print in mid-century, though there was no mention of a 'fine lady', and in a collection of rhymes printed in 1784 known as *Gammer*

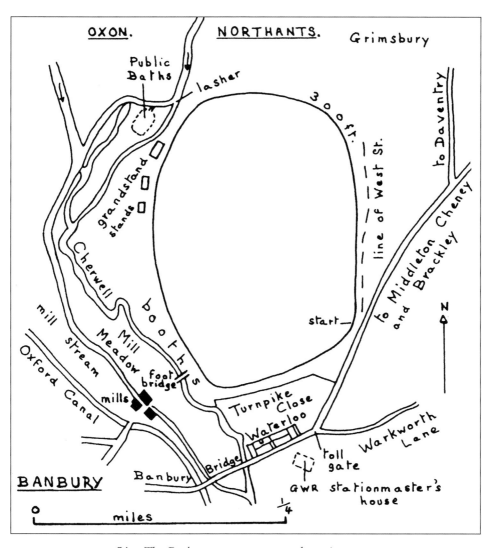

51 *The Banbury course was a popular racing venue.*

Gurton's Garland an old lady was riding the cock-horse. Since that time other publications of a similar kind have included variants of the best-known version:

> Ride a cock-horse
> To Banbury Cross,
> To see a fine Lady
> Ride on a white horse,
> Rings on her fingers
> Bells on her toes;
> She shall have music
> Wherever she goes.

The 'fine lady' made her first appearance in print in 1797 and many theories have been put forward about her identity. For a long time she was thought to be Celia Fiennes, a relative of the Wykham-Fiennes family at Broughton Castle. It is now appreciated that the nearest point to Banbury reached by Celia during her travels along the roads of the country was an unspecified part of Hertfordshire.

Despite the loss of the original crosses of the town in 1602, the rhyme persisted. The 'cock-horse' undoubtedly applied to hobby horses which were mounted by two persons, the man in front and the lady on a pillion behind. Brinkworth favoured the idea that riding a cock-horse, maypole dancing and the appearance of a lady on a white horse were all part of May Day festivities.[9] What is certain is that Puritan activity in the town put a stop to these forms of celebration and subsequent revivals have been related more to celebrations such as that when Queen Victoria's eldest daughter was married in 1859 or Victoria's Jubilees of 1887 and 1897.

One reason why the *Three Tuns* became such a notable inn was its possession of what was described as the 'Great Room'. This asset enabled the establishment to encourage business meetings such as those held about the canal, assemblies, balls, card parties and concerts. Its status was greatly enhanced by a position close to where annual horse fairs were held. These attracted at least one entry from each town or village within a radius of 15 miles, even though an average selling price of less than £8 per horse would seem to indicate 'rather ordinary all purpose animals sold to an indiscriminate local clientele'.

An important social diversion for people in the early 18th century took the form of horse races. These meetings were often impromptu affairs with few established rules but much money changing hands. Contests might involve just two horses or greater numbers of entrants. It was the upper classes who were the instigators of these events, but those of lower social status derived considerable entertainment value from

them. Evidence for racing at Banbury can be found in a list of 1727.[10] By this time Puritanism was waning and wealthy families like the Norths of Wroxton were emerging as potential patrons. Favoured locations are likely to have been pasture land near the hamlet of Neithrop or on Grimsbury Moors. The latter site was better known in the 19th century and was positioned on the Northamptonshire side of Banbury bridge. It was here that the Town Plate was run in 1720. A further 19 years of racing took place before the activity lapsed. The favoured years were 1720, 1727-9, 1734-6, 1738-9.

After 1739 and until the revival of racing in 1831 this form of entertainment may well have been stifled by renewed puritan activity, absence of patrons, lack of a venue or changing fashions. The revival of racing at Grimsbury from the early 1830s appears to have been associated with a better infrastructure for the sport; the course was longer and a grandstand was introduced.

Banbury also saw a succession of theatres.[11] The earliest of these, though not dated, was in the Horse Fair. It is was no more than a barn for strolling players and seems to have been located on the west side. Somewhere between 1798 and 1832 a man called James Hill erected a new theatre in Church Lane. This brick structure was capable of holding between 200 and 300 people. A Mr Henry Jackman was put in charge of the enterprise, which also included a touring company. The Jackman family was synonymous with theatrical activities not only in Banbury but right across the Midlands.

Six

GROWTH AND CHANGE
1800 TO 1900

The 19th century in Banbury was a time of growth and change. Traditional market town activities persisted and livestock continued to wander the streets but this was against a background of industrialisation and town expansion. At the beginning of the century the town was still governed according to the charter of 1718 but a series of Acts of Parliament abolished the Corporation and curbed the powers of the Justices, replacing them with a

system of government more representative of the population, or at least of the property owners.

The first improvement in the management of Banbury's affairs depended on the private 1825 Act for 'Paving, Cleansing, Lighting, watching and otherwise improving the several streets, lands, public passages and places in the Borough'. By the terms of this Act, 40 local commissioners were empowered to carry out the role of a town council. They had

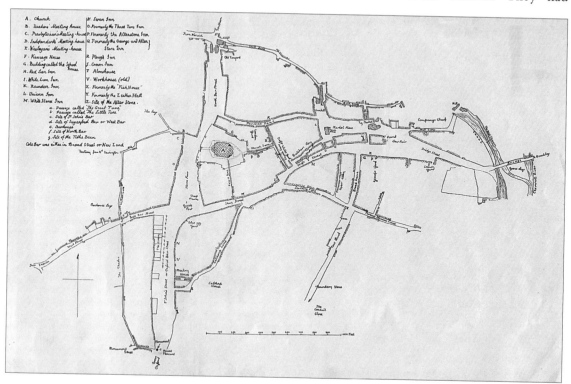

52 *The Davis map of Banbury 1825.*

53

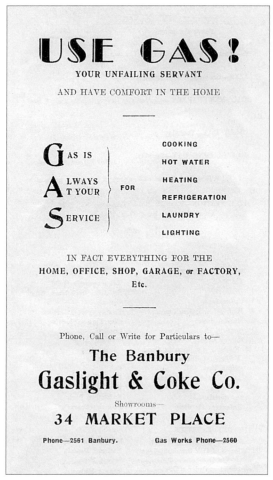

53 *Formation of the Gaslight and Coke Company presaged the transition from oil to gas lamps.*

responsibility for road repair, paving of footpaths, repair and erection of pumps, control of the borough stretches of turnpikes and the power to ensure that property owners drained their premises properly. Lighting was a concern of theirs and this meant oil lamps prior to the formation of the Banbury Gaslight and Coke Company in 1833. The Corporation and the commissioners were frequently at odds, especially on the issue of the erection of buildings.

Although both bodies were responsible for policing, Banbury was often an unsafe

environment because of the inefficient supervision of the watchmen, who failed to check the growth in robberies and cases of assault at the 12 annual fairs. To make matters worse, Neithrop was outside the scope of the watch and was rightly regarded as a disorderly suburb. In 1826 a mob uprooted trees which had been planted on the Green as part of an improvement scheme.

Reform measures of the 1830s brought considerable change to the pattern of local government countrywide. The Reform Bill of 1832 ended the Corporation's right to elect the borough Member of Parliament, and the Municipal Corporations Act of 1835 replaced it with a town council elected by ratepayers of the borough. The new council was to consist of 12 members, 4 aldermen and an annually elected mayor. When the first election took place on Boxing Day 1835, only 148 out of a possible 275 voters bothered to go to the poll. The outcome was decisive: 12 candidates each received over 100 votes whilst the remainder scored 11 or less.

The first members of Banbury Council

Timothy Rhodes Cobb	Banker	147
James Wake Golby	Attorney	145
Thomas Tims	Attorney	144
John Munton	Attorney	144
Thomas Golby	Carrier	144
John Hadland		142
Lyne Spurrett	Ironmonger	141
William Potts	Newspaper Proprietor	140
Thomas Gardner	Grocer	139
Richard Grimbley	Wine Dealer	138
James Hill	Builder	138
John Wise	Doctor	136

The terms of the 1835 Act meant that only Banbury came under the control of the new council. Hamlets like Grimsbury and Neithrop were excluded and did not even benefit from

ARTICLES AND RULES

OF AN

ASSOCIATION

FOR DEFRAYING THE EXPENSES OF APPREHENDING

AND PROSECUTING

THIEVES AND OTHER OFFENDERS,

IN

𝕭𝖆𝖓𝖇𝖚𝖗𝖞 𝖆𝖓𝖉 𝖎𝖙𝖘 𝕹𝖊𝖎𝖌𝖍𝖇𝖔𝖚𝖗𝖍𝖔𝖔𝖉.

———

ESTABLISHED JANUARY 1st, 1836.

———

𝕭𝖆𝖓𝖇𝖚𝖗𝖞:

PRINTED BY JOHN CHENEY, 6, BUTCHERS' ROW.

—

MDCCCLXXV.

54 *Title page of an original pamphlet of the Felons' Association 1875.*

	£ s. d.
Breaking or Damaging Windows, or Stealing any Doors, Window Shutters, Bars, Locks, or Bolts,	2 0 0
Stealing Poultry or Pigeons,	3 0 0
Stealing or damaging any Carriage, Waggon, Cart, Plough, or any Implement or Utensil in Trade or Husbandry; or any Iron Work belonging thereto,	2 0 0
Stealing, Cutting, Breaking Down, Burning, or Destroying any Trees, Evergreens, Shrubs, Hedges, Mounds, Fences, Gates, Stiles, Pens, Hurdles, Fleakes, Stakes, Pales, Posts, Rails, or any Iron Work, belonging to any Wood, Stealing any Grass, Corn, or Hay, either Growing, or in Shocks or Cocks in the Field. Robbing or Maliciously Damaging any Garden, Orchard or Fish Pond,	2 0 0
Pulling up, Stealing, or Destroying any Peas, Beans, Cabbages, Potatoes, Turnips, or other Vegetables, from the Fields of any Member,	2 0 0
Cutting any Mane or Tail of any Horse, Mare, or Gelding, or the Tail of any Bull, Ox, Cow, or otherwise Disfiguring them;	

55 *Extract from the list of rewards offered by the Association.*

the formation of a police force in 1836. Neithrop attempted to remedy this the lack by setting up the 'Neithrop Association for the Prosecution of Felons and other offenders'. Those who became members did so because they wanted protection for themselves and their property.

One of the areas of council responsibility that proved to be increasingly unsatisfactory was the town gaol. Between 1836 and 1852, when the gaol in the Market Place closed, the building was regarded as old and inadequate. And anyone committed for trial in Neithrop was taken to Oxford. In March 1851 the council considered a plan for a new gaol devised by Mr Walker, the current gaoler. A sub-committee appointed to consider it subsequently gave approval to the scheme, and the drawings were shown to Henry Underwood, an Oxford architect, who quoted £50 for preparation of plans and a basic sum of £3,800 for the construction. It was as well the council was taking this action because in April 1851 the Inspector of Prisons reported that he had not seen a gaol so bad.

Banbury Guardian reports of the time identify the proposed site as Parr's Piece in Calthorpe, which was beyond the borough boundary and

56   *The Old Gaol in Banbury Market Place was built in 1646 and remained in use as a prison until 1852.*
In the late 17th century the rooms above the cells were used as the Staple Hall for the town's wool trade, and from
1705 until 1817 the Blue Coat School was held there.

in the ownership to the Rev. Risley, but the location caused a great split of opinion. By May, other possible sites under consideration included Calthorpe Lane, Cornhill, Back Lane, Bridge Street and South Bar Street. A Mr Davies offered some land in the last of these areas, and Thomas Rhodes Cobb indicated his willingness for the site of the old workhouse to be used.

In 1852 the various proposals for a new prison were abandoned and the old gaol closed; the remaining prisoners were sent to Oxford. The funds reserved for the construction of the new prison were transferred to the new Town Hall, which duly opened in October 1854.

The canal extension from Coventry and its subsequent continuation to Oxford resulted in boat-related families basing themselves in Mill Lane, Factory Street and Cherwell Streets. These were highly mobile people as evidenced by a survey entry for 8 Cross Cherwell Street that referred to unnamed inhabitants as having 'gone boating'. The commercial value of the Oxford Canal, with its link to the port of London by way of the Thames Navigation, is very well illustrated in a series of letters written to a Mr Hartall of Shutford. In November 1815 John Williams of West Smithfield in London dispatched three chests of yellow soap to Paddington Wharf where they were collected by Pickfords, who had a regular fly boat service to Banbury. Thirteen years later Mr Hartall was still buying his soap from Williams, then of

Clerkenwell. A letter dated 28 August 1828 indicates a £27 14s. 2d. cost for chests of soap and the expense of transportation by, as before, the firm of Pickfords, who called at the Old Wharf in Banbury on Mondays, Wednesdays and Fridays according to Rusher's 1828 *List*.[1]

In all probability cargoes such as the yellow soap would have continued their journey to Shutford by means of the village carrier's cart. The carriers collected items of shopping for village customers, conveyed passengers for a small fee and transported goods for Banbury businesses throughout the 19th century. The thirty or so carriers named in *Rusher's List* of 1799 had grown to 208 carriers paying 465 visits to the town per week by 1838. They all developed good relations with local inns such as the *Leathern Bottle* and the *Old George*, whose yards received horses so that they could be fed and watered.

In the first half of the century passengers for other parts of the country relied on coaches and post-chaises. Advertisements in the *Banbury Guardian* illustrate the importance of the town to stage-coach travel. The appropriately named *Comet* ran by night. It left Leamington Spa at 5 p.m. and halted at the *White Lion* in Banbury's High Street at 9 p.m. It pursued its long and often chilly journey to the *King's Arms* in London's Holborn, arriving there at 9 o'clock the following morning. In 1838 a coach-railway service was established. The same Banbury inn was used by the Royal Mail coach that departed the town at 7 o'clock each morning and linked up with the Great Western Railway service operating from Wolverhampton to Paddington at Wolverton station at 10.30 a.m. The coach returned from Wolverton at 2.15 p.m. and reached Banbury at 5.30 p.m. thus allowing the journey to be made in the daytime.

In the early days of the railway companies the coaches were competitive. The *Sovereign* ran from Banbury to London at 'a very reduced

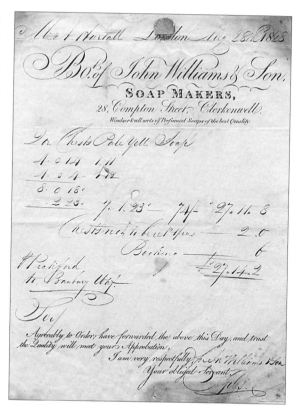

57 *Invoice from John Williams, London soap maker, to Mr Hartall of Shutford near Banbury.*

fare'. But coach journeys were often very uncomfortable. On Christmas Eve 1849, W.T. Henderson and William Cupitt, future Baptist minister and industrialist respectively, travelled with the *Union* coach from Tring in Hertfordshire to Banbury's *Red Lion*. The weather was extremely cold and the roads slippery, which meant progress was so slow that passengers travelling outside the coach could afford to walk for a distance sufficient to exercise their limbs. The route was by way of Windsor, Buckingham, Brackley and Middleton Cheney. From the top of Middleton Hill the lights of Banbury were faintly discerned.[2]

The coming of the railways in the 1850s enhanced Banbury's position as a major route

58 *The* White Lion Hotel, *popular with carriers.*

centre and gave industrialists like Samuelson the opportunity to reach markets more distant than those served by coaches or canal boats. The Great Western and the London and North Western Companies competed for passengers and goods. Local people could now explore beyond their own doorsteps. Advertisements in the *Banbury Guardian* for 9 April 1857 illustrate the battle for custom. Easter Holiday excursion trains were put on by both companies, who charged identical fares – 8s. first class and 5s. in covered carriages.

The GWR route was a branch from Didcot through Oxford, whilst the LNWR line connected Banbury through Brackley and Buckingham with the Bletchley to Oxford route at Verney Junction. Between 1850 and the end of the century two other lines extended Banbury's rail links. The GWR opened a line

to Kingham by way of Chipping Norton and the Grand Central Company provided a way to Woodford Halse.

Weaving of plush cloth, earlier known as shag, had become established in the previous century. Thomas Heath, who died in 1750, was registered as a journeyman and shagweaver, but parish records do not elaborate on the term 'weaver'. Occasional comments in newspapers like *Jackson's Oxford Journal* provide evidence of the success and profitability of the shag trade. John Newman claimed he had 'established the reputation of his own manufacturing in Banbury above that of any other' and that he had acquired a fortune of £50,000. This may help to explain how he was able to own the *Unicorn Inn* in the Market Place for a time.

The writer and traveller Arthur Young reckoned that by 1807 there were a thousand

59 *The* Red Lion – *right foreground.*

60 *The* Red Lion Hotel *interior.*

61   *The* White Horse Hotel *in the High Street – a popular venue for meetings and concerts.*

62   *The Great Western and the London and North Western railway stations in about 1854.*

handloom weavers employed in the Banbury area. The huge demand for looms was met partly by using oak rescued from St Mary's Church at the time of its demolition in 1790.

The story of plush making in 19th-century Banbury is one of company amalgamations and closures. Their changing fortunes can be followed in the pages of *Rusher's Directories*. In 1839 there were four firms: R. and T. Baughen of North Bar Street; Gillett, Lees and Gillett in the High Street; a Mrs Crosby occupying premises in Bridge Street; and Harris, Banbury and Harris also located in North Bar Street. That year marked the beginning of a decline in the industry locally. This was in part due to competition from plush weavers in the north of England, but power looms were also assuming importance and Banbury weaving was handloom-orientated. In the case of Gilletts' banking successes helped reduce the overall dependence on plush output and the name disappeared from the style of the firm in 1850. Baughens adapted to steam power in 1850 but suffered a factory explosion in 1859 and promptly closed. By the early years of the 20th century only one firm, Cubitt, Son and Co. (Cubitt, Wilson and Randall had taken over the business founded by Gillett, Lees and Gillett in 1861), remained. That closed in 1909, leaving companies like Wrenches to continue in the village of Shutford.

Corn milling, a feature of most market towns, was well represented in Banbury and District. Thomas Staley's mill was close to a mill-race offshoot of the Cherwell.[3] Staley dealt in coal as well as corn and his business boomed in the 1830s, when it was necessary for him to construct a warehouse on the western side of the nearby Oxford Canal so that he could take advantage of commodity movements by the various fly boats. Further evidence of the success of his affairs was the ability to afford a fine house in the elegant Horse Fair. However, in 1877 his company operations ceased and the mill was taken over by a firm called Edmunds and Kench.

Brewing was another typical market town activity but more widespread than milling in the 19th century. The Sun Brewery in Old Parr Road and Dunnell's Brewery close to the site of the north bar were relatively small enterprises compared with Hunt Edmunds and Co. Ltd, which was founded by Thomas Hunt. He brewed at the *Unicorn Inn* in the Market Place from 1832 to 1841 and was a maltster between 1835 and 1839, but had combined both activities by the time of the 1841 census. Seven years later the business embraced the *Unicorn*, a Bridge Street brewhouse and a malthouse in Parson's Meadow Lane. In 1850 came the highly significant partnership with

63 *The Sun Brewery, Old Parr Road.*

64   *Dunnell's Brewery, North Bar.*

65   *Hunt Edmunds Brewery in the town centre.*

William Edmunds, which brought about a progressive expansion of premises until 1866 when the adequacy of water supply for beer making became an issue. The company responded by acquiring springs and shallow wells in the Green Lane area of the town. In 1886 Hunt Edmunds had two breweries and 64 'tied' houses in Banbury. About this time bottling began on a small scale.

During the course of the century there was an increasing diversification of Banbury's industrial structure. On the northern edge of the medieval town, and next to Castle Street, a rope works was set up in the 1830s. Rusher's Trade Directories indicate this was in the ownership of several members of the Wall family, for whom location close to the Oxford Canal was crucial to the success of the business. A significant market was in cords necessary for the horse-drawn narrow boats. With Banbury at the centre of a major agricultural area, some heavy ropes were also required for tying sheaves of corn and hay to wagons.[4]

Another industry that boomed during this period but had a more widespread distribution was brick, pipe and tile manufacture. At a prime location in Grimsbury, between Duke Street and the Causeway, Lamprey and Sons had a large works of over 3,000 acres, which was based on an outcrop of Oxford Blue clay. Twelve thousand bricks a day were produced, but Lampreys were also known for pottery and tiles. In common with other 19th-century industrial enterprises in the town, there was speculative development of housing nearby. The company owned half of Duke Street and was responsible for the construction of 34 properties in Grimsbury. The Ordnance Survey map of 1882 reveals that bricks and their assorted products were made from Liassic clays quarried at several other locations. The chief of these were near Green Lane, on the southern margin of the Cherwell industrial area and close to the northern edge of Neithrop township, and two sites bordering the Broughton Road and to the west of the town. One of these, and now the site of a house called Old Quarry, was owned by Kimberleys, whose building activities played a prominent part in town expansion. The other and unrelated business was important enough to merit the construction of workers' cottages known today as Crouch View.

A consolidated area of industrial development appeared on the Cherwell

66   *A brick made by Lamprey's at their Grimsbury works.*

67   *Shop and home of the Lampreys in Bridge Street.*

meadows of south Neithrop during the second half of the 19th century. The flood plain became home to several companies and especially those connected with engineering. Undoubtedly the most important of these was the Britannia Works that Bernhard Samuelson expanded from an original implements business belonging to James Gardner in Fish Street. Samuelson had acquired much of his technical knowledge whilst in the Teesside area of north-east England and his determination to apply it in Banbury may well have been due to the town's increasingly focal position following the arrival of the railways.

Samuelson's operation was on two sites. An upper works bordered Britannia Road and included four fitter's shops as well as long machine shop bays. The lower works faced Swan Close and was developed during the major growth period between 1850 to 1870. At the outset 27 people were employed, but by 1849 nearly 300 worked for the company, most involved with agricultural implements that were exported to many parts of the world. With the depression years of the 1870s, however, diversification was necessary and products included power hammers, petrol engines and flour milling machinery.

In 1875 the need to speed up the movement of finished products from the two works to a lineside storage area meant the insertion of a light tramway, along which Samuelson's reaper binders began the first part of their journey to the grain lands of North America.

In explaining the great importance of the Britannia Works to Banbury's industrial history it is essential to acknowledge the technical and management support of people like Alexander and Ernest Samuelson, brother and nephew of Bernhard, and also David Pigeon. The turning point in the company's fortunes came during the following century. A serious fire in 1912 destroyed part of the Lower Works as well as some houses in Upper Windsor Street. The company was never the same after this. After a temporary closure in 1928, and a restructuring with new managers, the end came in 1933.

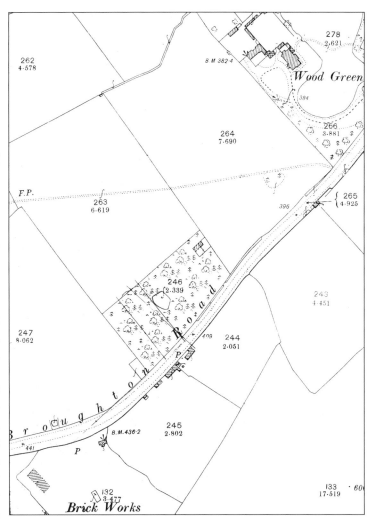

68   *Ordnance Survey map of 1899 showing Kimberley's brickworks near the Broughton Road.*

Thomas Barrow of Birmingham started another major engineering business in the Cherwell area in 1861. He formed an association with a man called Kirby who was experienced in steam engines and threshing machines and who had been in North Bar since the late 1850s. The outcome was portable and traction engines, threshing equipment, elevators, and steam-driven cultivating machinery. Then Barrow went into partnership with John Carmichael, who lived in Dashwood Road, and with William

Stewart. By the 1870s, 200 men were employed, making this the second largest engineering concern in the town. Late in the 19th century the firm decided to specialise in brass and copper engine parts.

The establishment of these major engineering industries between 1848 and 1861 in the south Neithrop area and in Neithrop hamlet created demands for labour that could not be met entirely from locally available workers. Barry Trinder records that 'less than

69   *Demolition of property in Bridge Street revealed a post-medieval ironstone structure behind later brick building.*

half of those employed in engineering in Banbury were born in the town'.[5] This led to a demand for housing and the Cherwell meadows area of south Neithrop was targeted by speculators such as Richard Gillett (former landlord of the *Crown Inn*), William Hobley and James Gardner, who employed builders to construct houses to rent wherever land prices were low. Streets such as Cherwell and Lower Cherwell were laid out to give access to these terraces, where rents ranged from £6 to £10 a year. By 1871 there were 350 dwellings in this area, of which 33 were in Windsor Terrace and occupied. This street was home to 17 skilled foundrymen.

The area as whole developed health and social problems because the land was ill-drained and Neithrop, which included the Cherwell area with a population of 4,000, was entirely without sanitation. Parts of the area were subject to periodic flooding. Many wells became contaminated and piles of filth appeared in the streets. A mid-century report by the Board of Health Inspector highlighted the ravages of illnesses such as cholera, and a fever described as the 'Banbury disease' was widespread.

After a series of cholera epidemics throughout the country in 1847 the government passed the Public Health Act of 1848, setting up a central Public Board of Health with the power to form local boards. The same report that highlighted the unsanitary state of the town recommended that the Act be applied to the whole ecclesiastical parish of Banbury, not just the borough – that is to say Banbury, Neithrop, Wykham, Easington, Calthorpe, Hardwick, Nethercote and Grimsbury. This was approved in 1852 and the whole area included in a

70 *Housing to rent, as in Lower Cherwell Street, followed in the wake of industry.*

drainage scheme, with sewers in Banbury, Neithrop and Grimsbury.

Banbury as a whole sustained population growth and was home to a thriving society based on a strong retail economy and a proliferation of inns. The Market Place was a heartland for taverns and the *Fox*, the *Plough* and the *Unicorn* were popular hostelries despite the nearby Victorian gaol and occasional disturbances at election times.

Around the 'leg of mutton' shaped Market Place and the nearer parts of Bridge Street, High Street and Parsons Street there was a large number of shopkeepers. In 1847 George Henry Baker was grocer and dealer in the Market Place, whilst R. Edmunds dealt in corn, seeds and hops at his Bridge Street premises. By 1871 there were 18 drapers in Banbury. Farmers continued to be Market Place orientated also.

The focal points provided by crosses, and especially the High Cross in Cornhill, were replaced by Corn Exchanges as places for buying and selling activities.

Expansion of the built-up area was evident in several other parts of Banbury. In 1836 Thomas Wall acquired several building plots along Back Lane, which connected North Bar Street with the Market Place. With the prospect of a new road, which became Castle Street East, 14 other pieces of land attracted interest, as did plots that were once part of a larger area known as 'Little Marsh' and which were offered for sale by Danby and Caless at an auction held in May 1863 at the *Reindeer*.

The break up of the Calthorpe Manor Estate led to further urbanisation. In 1833 Thomas Cobb, then owner of the manor, arranged for the estate of some 70 acres to be sold by lots at

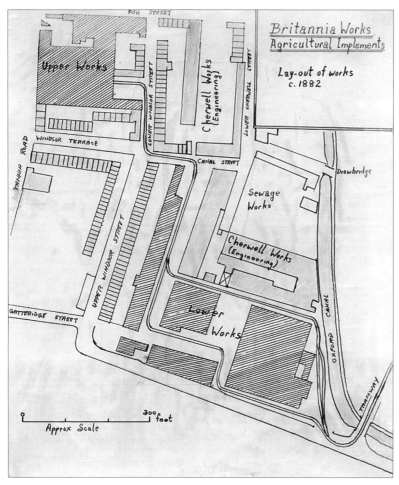

71   *Map of the layout of the Britannia Works in 1882.*

were considered appropriate for small houses, stables and gig houses. Immediately south of Upper Cross Road there were spaces in front of St John's Bar. The westernmost of these was auctioned on the basis that its perspective would command a pleasant view of the Green. In 1867 Thomas Orchard mapped out extensions to building land in Dashwood Road,[7] and several quality residences were constructed including Dashwood Lodge, which became home to William Edmunds in 1866 (brewer for Hunt Edmunds) and Arthur Stockton in 1901 (solicitor). They enjoyed the added advantage of a freehold enclosure with an orchard and a tennis court. At the eastern end of Dashwood Road, Thomas Orchard made provision for seven properties. The last of these, on the corner with Newland, had 'Public Elementary Day School' designation.

the *White Lion Hotel* in High Street. The estate included existing closes and cottages together with various plots of lands, as well as the large Windmill Fields to the east of the Oxford Road. This land was relatively high and dry, well away from the meadows near the River Cherwell where flooding was a periodic problem.[6] Plots with frontages on to St John's Street and with rear access to the Back Road were especially attractive for the construction of new buildings. At the time they were outside the borough of Banbury and not subject to the borough's taxes.

Further areas of land available between Lower Cross Road and the *Jolly Weavers Inn*

Some forty years on from Cobb's sale of Calthorpe House and Estate, Banbury was showing clear signs of expansion on its western edge and especially beyond the site of the West or Sugarford Bar. A fine terrace of Victorian villas was erected on the south side of West Bar Street in the early 1870s. Close by was the Shades footpath, which also bordered the very long and well-tended rear gardens of the mansions that faced the Green. Typical of these was Linden House, home to people of some status in the town. Miss Wyatt, who played a large part in the decoration of St Mary's Church in 1864, lived

72 *Photograph of Samuelson's men.*

there, and a later occupier was Charles Pemberton who occupied the post of surgeon at the Horton Infirmary.

In spite of the growth of population and settlement prior to 1889, Neithrop and Grimsbury were still villages in Oxfordshire and Northamptonshire respectively. Administration involved a complicated pattern of responsibility: Banbury Town Council performed the duties now carried out by the County Council in the borough of Banbury, the Oxfordshire County Justices assembled in Quarter Sessions to do the same for Neithrop and the Northamptonshire Justices for Grimsbury. The Board of Health was the only body acting for the whole area.

The case for an enlarged borough was a very strong one. It had often been discussed and proposals were put forward, but the delaying

factor was the cost of the necessary private Act of Parliament. From the mid-century Neithrop included a northern area around the Warwick Road and a southern section on the Cherwell floodplain where, as we have seen, the arrival of industry encouraged the construction of houses to rent. The rapidity of development was reflected in the population census returns. In 1841 Banbury, including Neithrop and Grimsbury, had a population of 7,241 people. Ten years later the figure had increased by 1,552 to 8,793.

In 1888 the Local Government Act transferred all the duties that had previously been carried out by Justices of the Peace, and many of those being carried out by Boards of Health and Education Boards, to elected County Councils. The Town Council acted at once to get the agreement of the new County Councils

73 *Photograph of the Cherwell industrial area showing the buildings and tall chimneys of the Britannia and Cherwell Engineering Works.*

74 *Walford's illustration of the Cornhill Corn Exchange.*

to alter the county boundary to include Grimsbury in Oxfordshire and extend the Banbury borough boundary to include the whole ecclesiastical parish. In July 1889 the order was granted and celebrated in some style with a peal of St Mary's bells, visits by the Volunteer Band and an evening torchlight procession to the accompaniment of more bell ringing and band music.[8] An important consequence was that the Town Council now administered the wider area in all aspects of policing and became the sanitary authority.

In the 1890s further development took place in and close to West Bar Street and its continuation, the Broughton Road, although in some cases there were restrictive covenants: 'No messuage ... shall be used as an Inn or Public House or Beer House and no bricks, tiles, pottery or lime shall be made or burnt thereon'.[9] A sale of 1897 reveals that much of the area near to the junction of West Bar Street and Bath Road had formerly been grassland with some associated spinney. Just over eight acres of it was known as the Flower Show Ground and belonged to William Munton, solicitor and also town clerk from 1850 to 1890. The name derived from William's habit of allowing the land to be the site of a huge annual show for the local horticultural society of which he was treasurer.

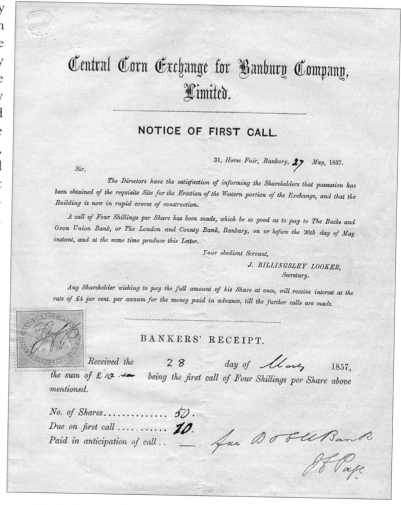

75 *Information for shareholders of the rival Central Corn Exchange.*

On the town side of these grassland areas, West Bar Terrace was at right angle to West Bar Street. Here there were four houses tenanted by Mr Washbrook, Miss Washbrook, Miss Stevens and Mr Webb. The adjacent 'West Garden' was rented by Thomas Smith who had it for £4 a year. Awaiting development in the 1890s was Berrymoor farm land. A typical sale lot consisted of two occupied cottages, each with a garden, as well as a rickyard and various farm buildings.

The link between properties of character and important professional people in 19th-century Banbury is well illustrated in the Horse Fair. In the 1860s No. 12 was occupied by Doctors Grimbly and Franly. Apart from the size and number of rooms there was the advantage of a well from which a wooden pipeline extended back towards the house and linked with a second well. Quality of life here was reflected in the way the gardens had been developed. The Ordnance Survey map of 1882 reveals that gardens were contiguous and no one was overlooked.[10]

At the beginning of the 19th century most people in the Banbury area still worked on the land or in trades and businesses in some way connected with agriculture. But things were gradually changing and the steady growth in population combined with jobs in the town put a strain on the machinery of local government trying to cope with a resultant increase in crime and poverty. Until the 1835 Municipal Reform Act the day-to-day administration of the borough was in the hands of the old Corporation.

Enclosure of land, changing farming practices, the mechanisation of trades such as weaving, improvements in the transport of goods and materials, and the return of soldiers after Waterloo meant that the numbers of poor in the Banbury area grew substantially. In 1833 the borough was required to raise £3,513 11s. 6d. from a population of 3,513 at the census of 1831.

Such was the outcry nationally that Parliament set up a Commission of Enquiry which paved the way for the Poor Law Amendment Act of 1834. Under this, parishes were grouped into 'Unions', each with a central workhouse governed by a Board of Guardians and under the control of the central Poor Law Commissioners. In addition to the borough, the Banbury union consisted of 50 other parishes, 35 in Oxfordshire, eight in Northamptonshire and seven in Warwickshire. The Banbury Board met for the first time on 6 April 1835. The venue was the old workhouse in South Bar but, unsurprisingly, the members withdrew to the more congenial surrounds of the *White Lion*. Early agendas focused on a new workhouse, and after examining various sites the Board members agreed to pay Charles Brickwell £1,050 for six acres of land at Neithrop. The building was erected by Danby and Taylor of Banbury and placed under the control of its first master and matron, Mr and Mrs Alexander Gate, in December 1835.

The workhouse was built to accommodate 300 inmates, with separate provision for men and women, boys and girls, so that families were broken up and had little on no contact with each other. The harshness of these conditions, coupled with the reimposition of the workhouse test for all able-bodied poor, made the 1834 Act very unpopular. Out-relief remained available only to the elderly and infirm. In Banbury their entitlement was 3s. a week for individuals and 4s. 6d. for married couples. Subsequently these arrangements were modified and a quantity of bread substituted for a proportion of the money. Threats to attack the workhouse were taken very seriously, and on one occasion (Michaelmas Fair Day in 1835) 50 special constables were stationed there.

The Act was successful in reducing the Poor Rate. Four years after its implementation, the level in Banbury had fallen from £3,763 13s. 10d. to £2,507 11s. 5½d. Due mainly to the severe winter of 1838, the number of paupers in the workhouse reached 282, the highest level since its opening. Out-relief increased during the early 1840s as more and more rural labourers were released from their jobs at a time when machines were replacing men on the land. An article in the *Guardian* in December 1842 observed that there was 'less reluctance to entering the workhouse than at one time appeared'.

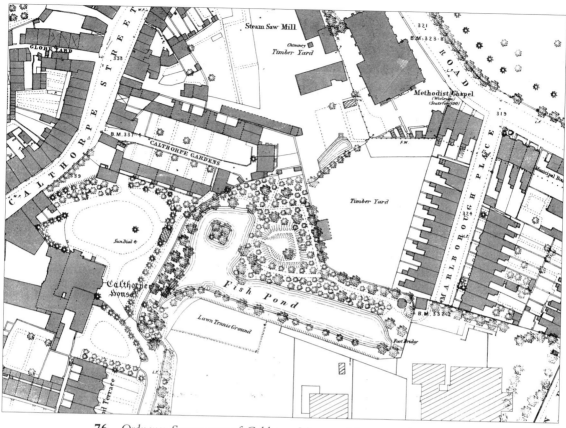

76 *Ordnance Survey map of Calthorpe Manor and its surroundings, 1882.*

77 *Calthorpe House and lake from a drawing by E.G. Bruton in 1852.*

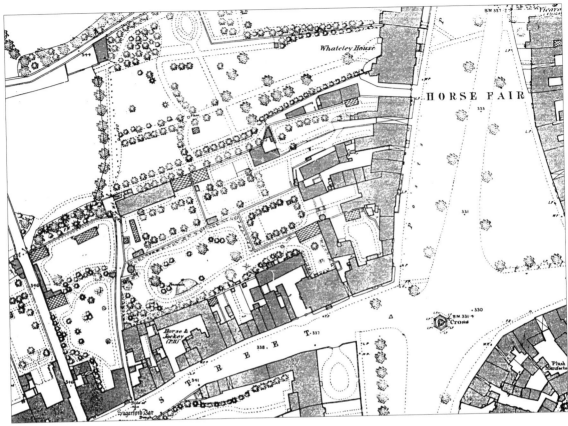

78 *Map of Horse Fair villas and gardens.*

Under the Municipal Reform Act the borough council had power to set up a police force for Banbury, and this was established in 1836 under a superintendent called William Thompson. He had responsibility for two full-time constables and the six watchmen who had been employed by the Commissioners under the old system. The first ever police station was in Church Lane, beneath the theatre, where it remained until 1854 when a base was set up in the new Town Hall. The jurisdiction of the Banbury Police did not extend beyond the borough boundary at the bottom of North Bar, so they were powerless to act in incidents such as the occasional protests against the introduction of new agricultural machinery. One of the worst cases took the form of riots and rick burnings

at Neithrop hamlet and in the nearby villages, and the task of dealing with the rioters devolved upon the Yeomanry. A hail of missiles from the rioters in the form of burning pieces of machinery caused their horses to bolt in terror back into Banbury and it was left to the more experienced 14th Light Horse Infantry from Coventry to quell the disturbances.

There was also a growing concern about vagrancy. Until 1838 a voluntary organisation called the 'Anti-Mendicity Society' had arranged to receive vagrants at a house near to the Bridge, but this house was closed in 1838, leaving the vagrancy problem to be tackled by the Board of Guardians, who made available tickets for admission to the workhouse where vagrants could receive food and, if required, medical

79 *Family wells were features of Horse Fair villas.*

attention. During the 1840s the arrangement was formalised by the establishment of what were called 'casual wards'.

People living in the rural parishes were unhappy about this way of dealing with the most severe cases of poverty. They felt they were paying a level of Poor Rate that was artificially high because of Banbury's problems. The *Banbury Guardian* came into being to explain the workings of the new Poor Law. In issue No. 1 William Potts, the editor, felt the workings of the Poor Law Amendment Act were not always well understood. In his opinion, the critical issue was the composition of the Board of Guardians and their public accountability. The need was for 'men whose eye is single towards the best interests of the labouring population'.

Visual impressions of the late 19th century were recorded by both local and national photographers but, before the era of the camera, the best insights into Banbury were conveyed in personal accounts. Sarah Beesley published a diary of recollections which she entitled *My Life*.[11] Sarah was the daughter of John Golby Rusher, a noted printer and Justice of the Peace. Born in Bridge Street in 1812, one of her earliest recollections of that street was a lack of light both inside and outside the house. Elections during the first half of the 19th century were also memorable, especially because of the custom of making beer available to the crowd who assembled at the Town Hall to hear results. In 1820, when the Hon. Heneage Legge became Member of Parliament, word reached the crowd

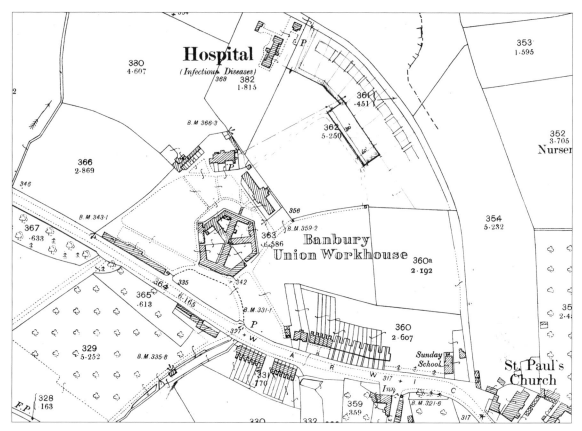

80   *Map of the workhouse near the Warwick Road.*

that ale was less abundant than usual. Stones were thrown and William Walford of the Corporation had to escape from the building and seek sanctuary in the *Plough Inn,* which was in Cornhill.

Sarah's family moved to a residence in the Market Place in 1832, most fortunately for them for a serious fire took hold of part of Bridge Street during 1859. It started in a large thatched building used as a warehouse by the village carrier, Golby. Sarah records that 'the fire caused a great deal of distress amongst the poorer classes whose homes were burnt down'. Strenuous efforts were made to control the blaze because of the proximity of property belonging to Hunt Edmunds Brewery. Fire engines attended from the borough of Banbury, Neithrop and Samuelson's Britannia Works.

The religious needs of people in Banbury were met in a diversity of establishments. Anglican St Mary's was much as it had been when rebuilt in 1797, although one man did bring about considerable change during the period 1860-81 and he was the Rev. Henry Back. Decoration of the ceiling and columns utilised money subscribed by Miss Wyatt of Linden House on the Green, and very tall piers were reduced in height. A total of £8,000 was spent during Back's ministry. Later additions to the furnishing of the church were an oak pulpit (1885) and wrought iron chancel gates (1902). The Diamond Jubilee of Queen Victoria in 1897 was celebrated with the installation of a new clock and quarter chimes with a carillon playing 21 tunes.[12]

81   *Crowds assembled at the Town Hall to hear the election results.*

A second ecclesiastical parish called South Banbury was set up in 1846. A significant reason for this development was the fact that St Mary's Church had very few seats for people who could not afford pew rents. Christ Church, which was consecrated in 1853, was a typical product of the Anglo-Catholic revivalism generated by the Oxford Movement.

The Roman Catholic church of St John's was built in 1838 on land released by the break up of the Calthorpe Manor Estate. Previously the Roman Catholics had used temporary accommodation in Red Lion Street.

The strength and diversity of nonconformity in 19th-century Banbury resulted in a surge of chapel construction. In 1812 the Wesleyan Methodists built a chapel in Church Lane, which

they sold to the Primitive Methodists in 1865 when they commenced activities in Marlborough Road. Wesleyan initiatives were also evident in Grimsbury, where a tiny North Street chapel was opened in 1858, to be replaced by the handsome West Street building in 1871. Schoolroom provision was made here five years later.

Congregationalists followed a very similar pattern of growth. A first meeting point in Church Passage dated from 1840, which was followed by the opening of a combined chapel and school in South Bar 16 years later. Plymouth Brethren took over the earlier building. The Baptist community were at an unspecified South Bar location in 1838 but developed a major chapel in Bridge Street three years later.

82 *Linden House (print of a water-colour by Pauline McTimony).*

83 *St Mary's Church before the building of Church House in 1904.*

Other groups in Banbury included the West Bar Calvinistic Baptists, voluntary led mission worshippers in the Warwick Road and a railway mission which opened near Grimsbury's Merton Street railway station. Unitarians, formerly Presbyterians, were in the Horse Fair from 1825. The oldest established place of worship was the Society of Friends' Meeting House in the north-west corner of the Horse Fair. Built in 1751, it was the home of a Banbury Meeting that served a wide area.

A milestone in the development of Banbury's institutions was reached in 1872 when the Bishop of Oxford opened the Horton Infirmary with its 20 beds and a dispensary. The founder was Mary Ann Horton of Middleton Cheney. Initially she gave some inheritance money towards the construction of almshouses, but

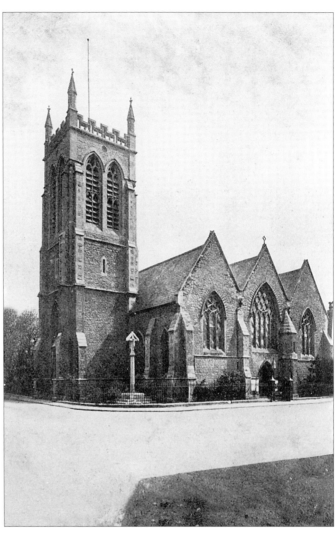

84 *Christ Church, South Banbury, opened in 1853.*

afterwards was determined to give Banbury people the gift of a hospital. Sadly, Mary did not live to see the realisation of her dream and it was left to her nephew John Henry Kolle to direct the family resources.

The dispensary made it possible for working-class people to obtain medical treatment by paying a weekly sum of 1d. per person or 3d. for a whole family. Patients could be recommended for treatment at the Horton by subscribing parishes or by people who had donated money to the hospital. Chief amongst the latter were M.P. Colonel North, Bernhard Samuelson and William Mewburn of Wykham Park.

Between 1875 and 1886 over £2,000 was donated, together with linen, cotton lint and bandages, and soon the Horton had more money than it actually needed for day-to-day running.

85 *St John's Roman Catholic Church was built in 1838.*

In 1897 a children's ward was made possible by the generosity of the Mewburns. It was their way of commemorating the Diamond Jubilee of Queen Victoria.

Prior to the creation of a National Board of Education in 1899, opportunities for education in Banbury were necessarily limited. In 1838 there was just one public elementary school and this was located in the Southam Road. The National Schools, founded in 1817, had by this time incorporated the Blue Coat Charity School, which dated from 1705 and was held in a room over the town gaol. Initially the trustees provided for as many children as their funds would allow. Their total costs for 1824 exceeded £83, of which £30 was for education and just over £30 went to cover a draper's bill for appropriate clothing.

Two British Schools were built and opened in Crouch Street in 1839, the second by the British and Foreign School Society for nonconformists, since separate provision was regarded as necessary for them. A logbook from 1890 to 1900 provides many valuable insights into the day-to-day operations of the British School for boys. Attendances were erratic, partly because poor road surfaces combined with adverse weather made it difficult for children from any distance to reach school. Other causes of unofficial absence related to family and social activities including club days, flower and fatstock shows and summer feasts in villages. Illness claimed its victims: influenza, measles and scarlet fever were scourges of Victorian England.

By the end of the century, school inspections appear to have been at least annual events. In 1892 reports on the boys school were complimentary: 'This school is in creditable condition and there is evidence of good and careful teaching.' However, by 1894 boys in the fourth standard were found to be backward in all subjects, and towards the end of the decade the inspectors became very critical of the building and its ventilation. Closure in 1900 could have been no surprise.

Neither of the Crouch Street schools catered for infants, who had to go to a building in Church Passage which was active from 1835 to 1868 and occupied a site at the rear of the *White Horse* yard. A committee of ladies was responsible for managing an establishment funded by voluntary contributions as well as by parents. Some 262 children were registered in 1840, but after 1846 figures did not include Roman Catholics, who went to St John's Day School set up by Dr Tandy.

The spectacular rise of an industrial suburb on the Cherwell meadows made it necessary to make some provision for the young children who remained in the locality. In 1851 an infant

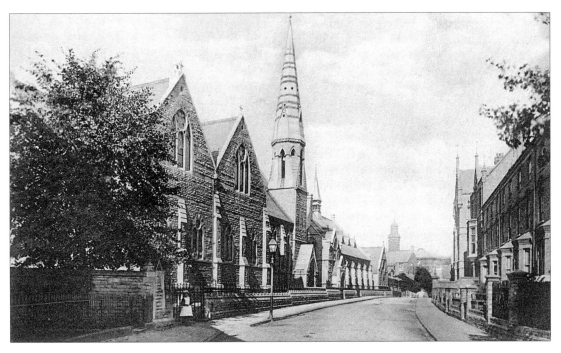

86   *Wesleyan Chapel, Marlborough Road, opened in 1865.*

87   *Children at Samuelson's Cherwell British Schools.*

88 *The Banbury and District Co-operative Society adopted Broad Street.*

school opened in Cherwell Street, a direct response to the expansion of the Britannia Works. Ten years later Bernhard Samuelson, owner of this business, paid for the construction of the Britannia British Schools (afterwards the Cherwell British Schools). By the end of the century, when school attendance had been made compulsory and fees abolished, over 400 children attended. Some families of Cherwell-based workers lived in Grimsbury and, to cope with this situation, Christ Church opened its National Schools in the Middleton Road in 1862.

Sunday schools played a crucial role in the education of many children in 19th-century Banbury. They were set up both by the established church and the nonconformists. By 1841 there were places for 300 boys and girls in the Wesleyan schoolrooms behind the

Church Lane chapel. In 1860 Christ Church in Broad Street opened a Sunday school for 200 children. These are good examples of the wider movement to set up opportunities for some form of education in Banbury and Grimsbury.

Adult education in the town was linked to the foundation of a Mechanics' Institute in Parsons Street and to its expansion at subsequent sites in Church Passage and, after 1884, Marlborough Road. The costs generated by the provision of and relocation to the last named site were met by Bernhard Samuelson. During the 1870s local classes were developed and their success led to the foundation of the Banbury School of Arts and Sciences. Mr J.H. Beale, headmaster of the Crouch Street Schools, had set about finding suitable teachers in 1863 with the help of like-minded people. His

89 *A Co-op float announces the Society's formation.*

90 *Banbury statistics and council officers at the end of the century.*

initiative was to prove highly significant as, in the 1880s, the Banbury School of Arts and Sciences was given accommodation on the upper floors of the Mechanics' Institute building in Marlborough Road. Mr Beale's son, Seymour H. Beale, was appointed headmaster. A few years later, in 1893, with generous financial help from Sir Bernhard Samuelson, a Secondary and Technical School building was built onto the Mechanics' Institute and, under the name of Banbury Municipal School, was opened with a register of 46 boys. Out of this development was to emerge Banbury Grammar School, a major provider of education in the town.

OFFICERS.

High Steward—The Right Hon. The Earl of Jersey, K.C.M.G.………

Recorder –The Right Hon. Alexander Staveley Hill, Q.C., M.P....£52 10s.

Town Clerk—Oliver James Stockton £300.

Clerk to the Justices—Charles Fortescue ……………………£210.

Clerk of the Peace—Daniel Pellatt...£18.

Surveyor and Inspector of Nuisances and Canal Boats—Nathaniel Holmes Dawson.......... ... .£200.
Office Hours—11 to 12 Daily.

Borough Accountant and Registrar of the Burial Board—T. Edwin D. Garrett …… ……………… ...£150.
Office Hours—10 to 12 and 2 to 4 Daily.

Medical Officer of Health— Innes Griffin ……………………£50.

Farm Manager—Geo. Sharp (with Residence, &c.) ….. ……………£100.

Seven

THE MARKET TOWN DIVERSIFIES
1900 TO 1945

Persistence of Victorian lifestyles was the hallmark of Edwardian Banbury. Photographs reproduced on postcards reveal the continuing dominance of carts in the Cow Fair and in the areas close to the Cross. The village carriers who accounted for many of these continued to regard Banbury as their metropolis.[1] Those shopkeepers who did not rely on the carriers had their own horse-drawn vehicles. Hunt Edmunds Brewery in the centre of town had drays to take beer to inns such as the *Dog and Gun* in North Bar. The change to motor traffic was slow, and childhood memories of the 1930s include the smell of steaming manure left by the huge dray horses that dragged wagon loads of barrelled beer to this part of town.[2]

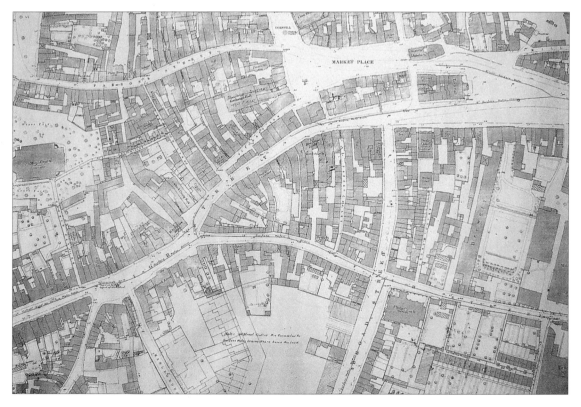

91 *Map of town centre, 1882.*

84

By the time of the First World War space on the roads was being shared with cars and motor cycles. Ewins Garage had 'Runabouts' priced at £115 and 'Five Passenger Touring Cars' at £125. They also hired out open cars, which were available at 6d. per mile. A rival company, Pytchley Autocars, offered vehicles with electric engine starter, dynamo and six lamps, together with the advantage of low petrol consumption. And George Ginger had become a local agent for Triumph, Douglas, Enfield and Scott motorcycles. His range of 1914 models included the speed machines of Triumph and Douglas and the two-stroke water-cooled Scott. Many town retailers were amongst his best customers.

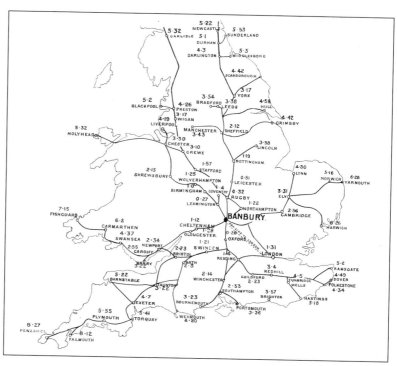

92 *Banbury had become an important rail centre by 1901.*
(Times are given in hours and minutes)

The Banbury in which these developments were stirring was very much a country market town. In 1901 G. Miller found the place 'a very picturesque town, then with its old houses and countrified appearance'.[3] However, not everyone in a population of some 13,000 was suitably accommodated. An undesirable legacy of Victorian times was slum housing, especially in south Neithrop near the canal and in Neithrop Township, whose spine was the present Warwick Road. In 1913 a reaction to the situation came in the form of 40 new council properties built on a King's Road site close to the Boxhedge part of the Township. This followed the 1890 Housing of the Working Classes Act.

The intervention of the First World War meant a delay to any further public sector developments until the mid-1920s and demobilisation of key people like Sydney Hilton, Borough Surveyor. Then 90 acres of Easington, in the south-west of the town, were developed for 400 houses, a public recreation ground and allotments. At the same time Edward Street appeared in Grimsbury. Private sector developments took place along the Oxford Road, Bloxham Road and on land between West Bar Street and the Bloxham Road.

Coincidental with this outward growth of the town came a movement to establish a form of public transport superior to most village carriers. In part this involved the replacement of carts by vehicles, which were especially converted for operation as buses. A good example was John William Sumner's Ford motor that was adapted by Simmons, coachbuilders in Bridge Street. John's 1926 bus had the discomfort of hard wooden seats but held more

93 *Carts continued to dominate the Cow Fair.*

94 *William George Dossett, Parsons Street grocer, in the Southam Road in 1900.*

passengers than his cart had during the journey from Hornton and Horley to Banbury.

However village pioneers like John Sumner were not alone. The Birmingham and Midland Red Omnibus Company timetable for 1924 reveals links to nearby villages such as Bodicote, Adderbury, Deddington, Bloxham and Hook Norton, but also to more distant and larger centres of population like Leamington Spa, Stratford-upon-Avon, Moreton-in-Marsh and Buckingham.

95   *Giles, the High Street butcher, also delivered by horse and cart.*

The centre of Banbury was still dominated by those family and local businesses that had flourished in the late Victorian town. Advertisements in publications like *Morland's Guide to Banbury and District* illustrate the nature and range of goods and services offered.[4] Arthur Pargeter, a Parsons Street tailor, proclaimed that ladies' costumes were 'a Specialité', and stressed that there were workmen on the premises. W.W. Trolley of Bridge Street manufactured 'the celebrated home-made pork pies'. Mrs A. Betts sold Banbury Cakes at her High Street shop and also at the Great Western railway station. Her new tearooms in the town were said to be 'central and convenient for ladies, cyclists and travellers'.

By the end of this period great changes were under way in the retail trade of the town and branches of chain stores were gradually replacing the individual private traders in the High Street. Boot's Cash Chemists and W.H. Smith & Sons were both well established before the First World War, but the most significant change to the middle part of the High Street was the demolition in 1930 of the *Red Lion*, an old coaching inn, to make way for F.W. Woolworth & Co. Ltd. The firm's arrival was seen as a retailing revolution. With its attractive pricing strategy it was known as the '3d. and 6d. store'. Woolworth's was followed in 1934 by Montague Burton's chain tailoring business, which came to occupy the site on the corner of Butchers Row. This had been the *Criterion Inn* and, latterly, the fruit and vegetable enterprise of Harry Boxold.

The inter-war period also saw branches of the 'Big Five' national banks establishing themselves in the High Street and adjacent areas.

96   *William Truss of Parsons Street was a fishmonger who replaced his cart with a modified Ford-T vehicle.*

At the beginning of the Victorian era Banbury had been served by three banks set up by local businessmen – Messrs Timothy Rhodes and Edward Cobb (the Old Bank) in the High Street, Messrs Joseph Ashby Gillett and Henry Tawney in Cornhill, and the Leamington Priors and Warwickshire Banking Company in the Market Place. Managed by Mr William Fairbrother, a linen draper, the latter had ceased trading in Banbury by 1848. The first of the big names to appear was Lloyds in 1902, which amalgamated with Messrs Cobb. Messrs Gillett and Tawney's bank merged with Barclays in 1919, moving to new premises at the corner of Broad Street in 1934. An early arrival in the High Street, in 1846, the London and County Bank, had, after various name changes, become known as the Westminster Bank by the inter-war period. In 1882 the Birmingham Banking Company

opened a branch at 95 High Street. It changed its name several times before moving to reconstructed premises at 10 High Street in 1916, when it was known as the London, City and Midland Bank, a title that was later shortened to Midland. The last of the 'Big Five', the National Provincial, opened a branch on part of the *Red Lion* site. In addition, in 1939 the District Bank started up next to the Westminster, thus doubling the total of banks over a period of 100 years.

Meanwhile Broad Street was the scene of an exciting new venture by the Banbury and District Co-operative Society, the town's first ever shopping arcade. The previously separate departments were rehoused in one building and a 'cosy corner café' was added. On the opening day in 1934 people thronged to Broad Street to welcome a 'miniature Selfridges'.[5]

A less happy situation existed in Bridge Street, where there was growing awareness of the need for improvement to an important 'gateway' to Banbury. The Bridge Trust of Banbury Charities administered much of the property, which aided the plan to improve frontages and develop shops. An Oxford architect by the name of Thorpe was commissioned to prepare an overall plan. Once accepted by the council, work proceeded slowly but it included some significant motor trade activity on behalf of Trinders and Whites. The way was paved for the Trinder development by the termination of a lease held by a Mr Davies who had become involved in the unpopular practice of bill posting in nearby Lower Cherwell Street.[6]

Farming was still the single most important occupation in inter-war Banbury and District. Agricultural markets occupied the streets and open spaces until the mid-1920s. Sheep continued to be penned in the Horse Fair, whilst drovers brought cattle to the Cow Fair which was just east of the Town Hall. But the notable increase in motor traffic after the First World War meant the street market was becoming impossible. There was also growing concern about public health as well as pressure to clean up the town. In January 1919 A.T. Johns, who was Medical Officer of Health for Banbury, used his annual report to underline the need to halt livestock sales in the central area. He also wanted a public abattoir and cold store in place of the private slaughterhouses such as those of Mary Gascoigne in Castle Street West, William Trolley in Mill Lane and William Jelfs in North Bar Place.

The answer to his concerns came in 1925 in the wake of Banbury Borough Council's purchase in 1919 of garden ground for the establishment of a centralised market. Their choice of location was close to the junction of the Southam and Warwick roads. The 6½ acre

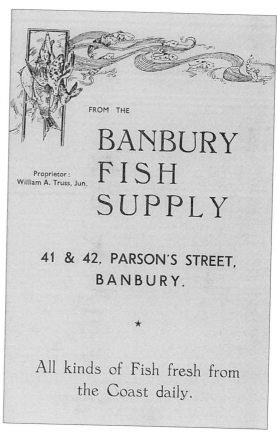

FROM THE

BANBURY FISH SUPPLY

Proprietor:
William A. Truss, Jun.

41 & 42, PARSON'S STREET, BANBURY.

★

All kinds of Fish fresh from the Coast daily.

97 *Advertising card for Truss, fishmongers.*

site cost £2,200 but did not satisfy the farmers, who wanted to be near to the railway. An inspector at the Ministry inquiry decided in favour of the farmers and a syndicate was formed headed by A.P. McDougall, which evolved into Midland Marts Ltd. At first only sales by auction took place on the new site, the dealers' market being left in the town centre, but growth of the business brought more traffic to the town and it became evident that livestock sales in the town centre would have to cease. In 1931 all transactions were transferred to the new market site. The move was not popular with everyone, especially those town centre retailers who feared loss of custom from the farmers, but their concerns proved groundless and the new market

98   *Ewins produced trade cards to promote their early model cars.*

grew in importance so that by the end of the 1930s stock was going to 31 counties.[7]

The 1930s were also a time of improvement for town roads. Varying sums of money were offered by the charter trustees towards the cost of widening Castle Street, Upper Cherwell Street, North Bar Street and, in Grimsbury, Middleton Road, Merton Street and the Causeway.[8] There were also entirely privately funded enterprises. An important example, because of the proximity of the Horton Hospital, was High Town Road.

Despite its image as a market town Banbury had a variety of industry that provided a significant employment base. Samuelson's Britannia Works continued to dominate the Cherwell area, though a serious fire in 1912 had damaged one of his factory complexes as well as setting light to some nearby houses. The company was never as vibrant again.

As Bernhard Samuelson was winding down his operation, an Alkerton farmer by the name

of Henry Owen Bennett was planning to use St John's works in St John's Road for the manufacture of ladies knitwear. The building had previously been a malt house for the Sun Brewery, which was located in Old Parr Road. In 1927 a firm called Spencer Corsets Ltd took over the Britannia Road factory of Messrs W.F. Lucas & Co., who had been manufacturing ladies' linen underclothing on the site since 1896. They became renowned for special appliances and corsetry of all kinds and were widely recognised as a paternalistic company. Employees were encouraged to take advantage of social and sporting opportunities. From 1932 until the mid-60s, Banbury Spencer FC was the town's football team, their gold and red shirts earning them the nickname of 'The Gay Puritans'.

Switchgear and Equipment Ltd grew out of the need for electrification in the Banbury area in the 1930s. Its establishment also met an urgent need for jobs following the closure of the Britannia Works. In fact, expansion beyond

TELE GRAMS: "EWINS, BANBURY."
PHONE: No. 11.

EWINS & SON

Coach and . .

Motor Works.

Works :—MARLBOROUGH PLACE.

Office :—31, HIGH STREET.

CARS FOR HIRE

TROLLEY & SONS

PORK BUTCHERS,

Pastrycooks & Confectioners,

92, High St. & Bridge St., BANBURY.

MANUFACTURERS OF THE
CELEBRATED PORK PIES,
SAUSAGES,
AND
BANBURY CAKES.

Dining & Refreshment Rooms
HOT JOINTS DAILY.

MAKER OF ALL KINDS OF CAKES & PASTRIES,

HOT AND COLD BATHS.

92, High St. & Bridge St., BANBURY.

MRS. A. BETTS,

Banbury Cake Maker
and
Confectioner,

85, High St., Banbury.

Bride, Lunch, Madeira Cakes, &c.,
ALWAYS ON HAND.

POUND, CHRISTENING, AND OTHER CAKES
Made to Order.

99 *Sequence of advertisements − Ewins, Trolley and sons, Mrs A. Betts.*

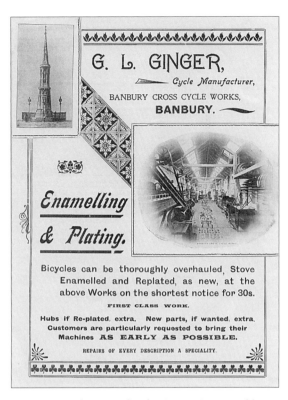

G. L. GINGER,
Cycle Manufacturer,
BANBURY CROSS CYCLE WORKS,
BANBURY.

Enamelling & Plating.

Bicycles can be thoroughly overhauled, Stove Enamelled and Replated, as new, at the above Works on the shortest notice for 30s.

FIRST CLASS WORK.

Hubs if Re-plated, extra. New parts, if wanted, extra. Customers are particularly requested to bring their Machines AS EARLY AS POSSIBLE.

REPAIRS OF EVERY DESCRIPTION A SPECIALITY.

100 *An advertising flier for George Ginger and his cycle business.*

the original capacity meant that in 1937 the firm occupied part of Samuelson's former Lower Works. A year later Switchgear was on the move again, this time to the Southam Road where the company found an appropriate site.

Industrial survival in the late 1920s and '30s was never easy, yet it was essential for the health of a town in which unemployment was so severe that William Truss, the Parsons Street fishmonger, gave away bags of potatoes at the door of his shop. Closure of Samuelson's Britannia Works in the early '30s threatened a black future for the town, but negotiations between the Northern Aluminium Company and Banbury Borough Council resulted in a sheet mill, employing some 200 people and capable of producing up to 200 tons a month, being erected on a 40-acre site in the Southam Road in November 1931. The effect on the unemployed register in Banbury was immediate: in December 1931 1,254 people were listed; in the same month in 1932 the figure had dropped to 981.

101   *Red Cross nurses at the GWR. station. They had a hospital in Grimsbury.*

Early years at the factory were characterised by conflicts between management and workforce.[9] This culminated in a strike followed by a protest meeting attended by 1,600 people in the Market Place on a Sunday evening in 1935. At stake were a wage increase and the right to form a branch of the Transport and General Workers Union. The strike was over in a few days. Gains were few in number but by 1940 a 1d. an hour increase had been negotiated and a ban on smoking relaxed. A further

102   *Palmer and Son had a wharf in Lower Cherwell Street.*

necessary improvement forced upon the company in the Second World War was the setting up of day nurseries so that married women could work.

Despite the difficult start, the company's presence in Banbury had a number of beneficial effects over and above the increased employment opportunities. Its participation in the annual Horton Hospital fete greatly boosted the fund-raising activities. In 1939 the fete showed a profit of £684.

The two world wars had a considerable effect on industry and employment. During the First World War a Grimsbury-based National Filling Factory was set up because the area was seen as remote from parts of the country susceptible to attack. Women earned an average of 25s. 9d. per week filling shells with chemicals which turned their skins yellow and gave rise to their nickname, 'Canaries'. The Oxfordshire Ironstone Company opened up a quarry face in the Wroxton area and moved the stone to the main Great Western Railway by constructing a branch line.

103   *The* Red Lion *ready for sale.*

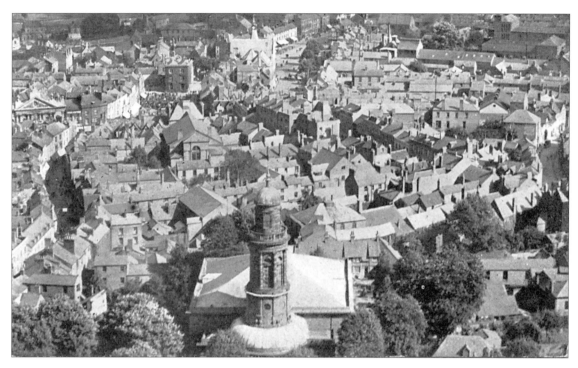

104   *Aerial view of Banbury, looking east from St Mary's Church in 1920.*

105   *Aerial view of the Green, Cross and Horsefair in 1920.*

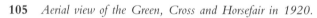

106   *Staff of Hood's Ironmongers, Bridge Street. A mobile advertising unit in front of the shop in the 1930s.*

107   *Brown's Cakeshop card to announce the opening of their Christmas showroom in Parsons Street.*

108   *Brown's presentation pack for the visit of Queen Elizabeth II in 1959.*

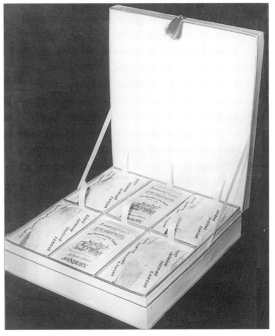

109   *Aerial view of part of the Calthorpe area, south-east of the Cross, c.1920.*

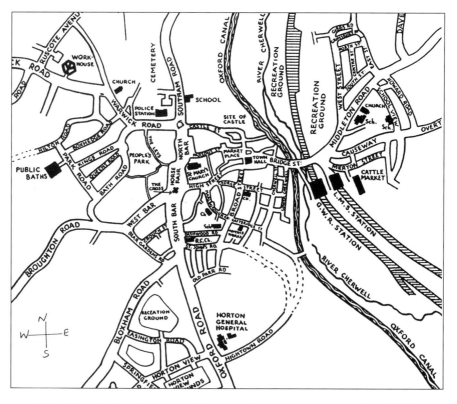

110   *Map showing the layout of Easington (south-west corner) in about 1930.*

Leisure needs in Edwardian Banbury were served by the opening in 1906 of Blinkhorn's 'Picture Palace' in what had been a failed corn exchange of the previous century, and by the appearance of the Grand Theatre in Broad Street five years later. For those more interested in exploring the surrounding area there were several country walks beyond the built-up area. Six of these led towards Broughton, Burton Dassett, Horley, Wroxton, Wykham and Overthorpe.[10] Adjacent to the town were rights of way across the fields. Between West Street (now West Bar Street) and Bath Road are a series of footpaths called the Shades. Perceptions of them varied with the nature of the surroundings as well as the weather. The section nearest the Clap gate exit on to Bath Road was known as the 'Crooked Shades'. In a letter to Oliver Stockton, the

111   *Aerial view of Midland Marts stockyard.*

Town Clerk, William Orchard, who was a local property owner and builder, described the Crooked Shades as 'that objectionable dark place'.[11] In 1903 the residents of Bath Road, Bath Terrace and Queen Street unanimously supported his proposal for a properly made up diversion.

The recreational facilities of the town were greatly improved by the opening of the Peoples Park in 1912. A deferred legacy from George Ball, a Parsons Street pharmacist, enabled a

syndicate to purchase Neithrop House and grounds and public subscriptions enabled the site to be secured and used as a public park until the legacy became available in 1917. The Town Council took over the park, which was officially opened as part of the peace celebrations in 1919. During the inter-war years various facilities were added which enhanced its attractiveness. The condemnation of some old cottages known as Paradise Square enabled the council to increase its size and provide land for hard tennis courts,

112 *A sheep auction in progress at Midland Marts livestock market.*

113 *Before and after the war the Christmas Fat Stock Show was a major event. Here the Mayor of Banbury in 1957, Councillor Malcom Spokes, presents a £50 cheque to Mr. A.H. Lovell, owner of this champion Aberdeen Angus steer.*

a bowling green, a putting green, an aviary, a children's playground and a paddling pool. In October 1931 a gift enabled the replacement of a rudimentary structure with a substantial bandstand. As noted above, a large area of ground at Easington was set aside for recreational use as part of the post-First World War housing development, the aim being to provide pitches for those who wished to play organised games but could not afford to hire a private ground.

Land was also acquired in Grimsbury. In March 1932 the Bridge Trustees acted as intermediaries between the Great Western Railway and the Town Council in the acquisition of some valuable land near the *Elephant and Castle*, just south of the entrance to the Causeway. Nine months later a grant of £200 from the railway company enabled the council to purchase six acres of land between West Street and the railway from the Rev. Hartley. The area came to be known as Moorfields and was set aside by the Corporation as a recreation ground for Grimsbury. This was in compensation for the removal by the Great Western Railway of a footbridge, which had allowed the people of Grimsbury access to the borough recreation ground on the other side of the line.

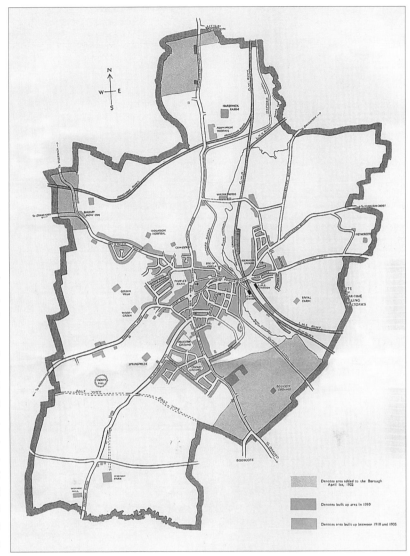

114   *Sketch map of the Borough of Banbury, 1935.*

On the western side of Banbury steeplechasing was established on and around Crouch Hill. The races were held under National Hunt rules and attracted entries from all over the country. At each meeting there was usually one locally orientated race.

The Silver Jubilee of George V and George VI's accession to the throne in 1937 were the occasions for street parties. On 6 May 1935 the

115   *Residents of Calthorpe Street celebrate the 1937 coronation in some style.*

116   *John Cheney, Mayor of Banbury, visits the 1937 coronation tea party for Calthorpe Street children.*

Jubilee was celebrated with band concerts, games and sports for children on the Harriers and Easington Recreation Ground, as well as activities in the People's Park that included a film show of events in the town during the 25 years of the reign. It concluded with a fireworks display. Celebrations for the Coronation were on an even grander scale. A *Banbury Guardian* report of festivities in the Cherwell Streets records that E.W. Brown, the Banbury Cake firm, provided tea for the children, whilst one of the departments of the former Britannia Works was the venue for a supper for adults. 'Flags and numerous other devices were suspended across the road and the houses were bedecked with national emblems and photographs of the King and the Queen.'

With the outbreak of war in 1939 Banbury's reputation as a safe haven won it large numbers of evacuees from the London area. Both the Northern Aluminium Company and Spencers became involved in work connected with production of the Spitfire aircraft. Assembly lines were staffed largely by female operatives and the NAC survived the few local bomb incidents by creating a dummy factory nearby. By contrast, the gasworks close to the Great Western railway line suffered a direct hit.

VE and VJ Days were celebrated in some style. Street parties were common across the town, and extant group photographs testify to the feeling of relief and the knowledge that, despite the departure of warm-hearted American

117   *Banbury Spencer F.C. was recognised as the town club between 1932 and 1966.*

service personnel and the inevitable austerity, Banbury was ready for a new future. This arrived in 1952 when Banbury Borough Council and the London County Council agreed that the town of cross and cakes should receive overspill population.

118   *Aerial view of Banbury, 1929. The Cherwell industrial area and canalside development occupies the foreground. The Market Place and Bridge Street are clearly visible in the centre. The Castle Gardens are centre background, bordered by a wide arc of the Oxford Canal.*

119   *Northern Aluminium Company works early in the 1930s.*

Eight

POST-WAR DEVELOPMENTS
1945 TO 2002

The Banbury that emerged from the war years was not much changed from the town of 1939. Bomb attacks had been limited to sites such as the gasworks and the dummy factory that had been constructed on Hardwick Hill to draw attention away from the true scene of operations. During the war the NAC contributed significantly towards Spitfire production and even added a melt down unit at Adderbury to the south of the town. It was here that the remains of crashed aircraft were handled. The many evacuees from London included the pupils of Fulham Girls and Bow Central School, who shared the Easington premises of Banbury Grammar School.[1]

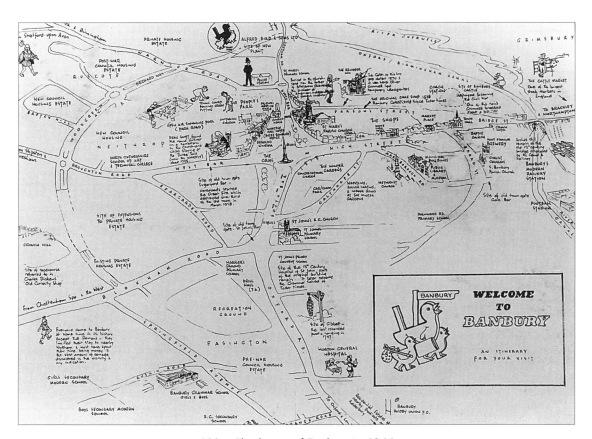

120   *Sketch map of Banbury in 1966.*

Even allowing for the war's disruption, it is now difficult to appreciate how local and insular life was in the 1940s and 1950s in a town led by its mayor and Borough Council. The first population census after the war, that of 1951, indicated growth of 6,000 people since the previous count in 1931. This reflected the persistence and expansion of the aluminium industry, which now included provision for research. In 1938 Aluminium Laboratories Ltd built premises opposite the Northern Aluminium Company Works and these were requisitioned for Ministry war offices soon after the outbreak of hostilities.

The year 1951 was notable for a highly successful Industrial Exhibition held in St Mary's Church House and on a nearby part of the Horse Fair. The event marked a turning point in Banbury's history. The Hunt Edmunds Brewery stand boasted that roughly thirty delivery vehicles served seven counties. In 1967

121 *Another tanker leaves Hunt Edmunds Brewery in Bridge Street.*

Hunt Edmunds' associated properties were sold,

122   *The end of an era as Hunt Edmunds Brewery chimney falls.*

the public houses to Mitchell and Butler and the hotels to Bass Charrington. Seven years later the landmark brewery chimney was toppled. Only attractive plaques on some inns like the *Blarney Stone* remain as evidence of brewing.

Following the Town Development Act of 1952, the Borough Council signed an 'overspill' agreement with London County Council. Banbury joined the ranks of Britain's 'expanding towns' and the Bretch Hill Estate was built, where houses for Londoners were linked to the relocation of industries away from the capital. Elsewhere in the district, central government and developers have been the guiding forces. The town has advanced into the surrounding countryside and high-density infill in villages like Middleton Cheney, just east of Banbury, have provided much sought-after rural retreats.

Despite the policy change, traditional influences still persisted. In 1956 nearly 219,000 animals changed hands at Midland Mart's livestock market. The importance of these sales

was illustrated by the *Farmers' Weekly* magazine for 9 August 1957, which observed that 'the growth of this market since the 1920s has been unparalleled anywhere in the country'.[2] With the opening of the M40 motorway in 1991, it seemed inconceivable that Banbury's livestock market should not have had a long period of sustained development, but closure was announced seven years later and saddened farmers came to the stockyard for a sale of effects in June 1998.

The nearby railway lines were busy in the 1950s with freight and passengers. Hundreds of wagons could be seen in Banbury's huge marshalling yard and by 1955 rebuilding of the old Great Western station was under way. During the following decade Banbury suffered its share of the Beeching cuts. In 1964 the Banbury to Buckingham line out of Merton Street station closed, and two years later the town's link with the Great Central main line at Woodford Halse was severed and the steam

123 *Memories of steam at Banbury's Merton Street station.*

124 *Diesel trains were a mid-1950s attempt to keep the Buckingham line alive.*

locomotive depot shut. The replacement diesels were housed nearer the station, but even that depot ceased to function in 1984. The 'hump' marshalling yard was not operational beyond the start of the seventies.

A renaissance for the railways locally has had to await the operations of the Chiltern, Thames and Virgin companies. The new Turbos and Voyagers, a doubling of the track between Banbury and Bicester and the prospect of a future bus/train interchange may offer the chance of a new dawn.

The Oxford Canal continued to feature in the life of the area, though less for commercial and more for leisure activities. By the 1960s coal traffic was very limited, mainly serving the nearby Unigate Dairy which was still dependent on fuel from the Warwickshire mines. By contrast, there was a surge in pleasure craft numbers from 600 in 1947 to 6,000 in 1955.[3]

The Education Act of 1944 led to a complete reorganisation of provision in the town in the immediate post-war years. But it also meant the loss of local control. Existing schools could not cope with the new demands and an expanding

125 *Addison Road with Blessed George Napier School at the far end.*

126   Above: *1930s art room of Banbury Grammar School*. Below: *by the early 1990s the same room had become the European Business Centre of Banbury School.*

127 *This engineering workshop symbolises the past importance of technical training at the North Oxfordshire College.*

school population. New primary schools were built in the developing areas of the town. Harriers Grounds Primary School was opened in 1949, closely followed by Neithrop Infant and Junior in 1951. Further population pressures in the 1960s led to the opening of Hill View County Primary and Queensway School. A Secondary Modern School for boys adjacent to Banbury Grammar School in Ruskin Road, Easington was opened in 1952 and a girls' school on the same site in 1957. Grimsbury made its own provision. In 1962 a Roman Catholic Secondary School, the Blessed George Napier, opened to its first 171 pupils. The North Oxfordshire Technical College and School of Art had transferred to its Bath Road site by 1961.

As early as 1962 discussions had begun to radically overhaul the secondary system and within four years Banbury School had been established. The schools on the Ruskin Road Campus and one in Grimsbury became a federation of halls, with a separate upper school and close links to the Technical College. A common programme and timetable made it possible for school- and college-based students to study for similar 'A' levels and for the latter to follow more vocational routes, such as Ordinary National Diploma. A key figure in the reorganisation was Dr Harry Judge, who became Principal of Banbury School and was responsible for the education of over 2,000 pupils in 1967. A new comprehensive, Drayton School, was built on the northern edge of the town in 1973.

By 1977 major changes to secondary education were again under discussion by a county council 16-19 working party. Most controversially, these included a new sixth form centre for the whole of north Oxfordshire at Banbury School, drawing pupils from Drayton,

128   *Students dressed as Pentonville girls at North Oxfordshire Technical College Rag Day, 1967.*

the Warriner School at Bloxham and the Blessed George Napier School, all of which had hoped to establish their own sixth forms. Only the Blessed George Napier was allowed to develop independently.

In the 1960s a second wave of migrants entered the town, this time from Digbeth, Birmingham, in the wake of a decision by Alfred Bird and Sons of Deritend, the renowned dessert foods manufacturer, to leave the West Midlands after 125 years. Despite government pressure to relocate to a Development Area, the General Foods Corporation of the United States (owners of Birds) chose a 31-acre site at Banbury because it was not remote from Birmingham, would allow consolidation of existing operations and, above all, permit new product line growth. An important feature of the development was a coffee-making plant. Maxwell House Instant Coffee had become a major brand for General

Foods in the late 1950s. In 1963 the company promised work for all employees willing to move to Banbury and, possibly, for those in London still seeking houses under the overspill agreement.

The contract with General Foods was a highly significant achievement by Banbury Borough Council and was all the more remarkable because of the state of full employment at that time. The company move followed on the heels of Automotive Products Limited of Leamington Spa, whose Spares Division opened in December 1962 with a workforce of over 700.

Selection of Banbury by both companies fitted neatly into plans for the expansion of Banbury's population from 20,000 to 40,000 by 1980. The Borough Council's task was certainly helped by remarks such as those of John Davis, Birds Community Relations Officer,

129   *Frank Toole's cartoons appeared in* Banbury News *– a General Foods Publication.*

130   *Brown's Cakeshop was an essential part of the Parsons Street scene.*

who described Banbury as 'a very pleasant, progressive and prosperous little town'. No wonder General Foods had selected it from a short list of 100 possible locations.

The £6 million factory was completed during 1965. Two years later the town was in the news again but this time there was no cause for celebration. Brown's renowned shop in Parsons Street, where Banbury Cakes had been baked since the 17th century, was sold to Courtenay Investments of London, who demolished it despite desperate attempts to prevent them. The magazine *Country Life* noted that, 'stopping the demolition alone is a Pyrrhic victory for those who care about Banbury's history'.[4] Many held on to the hope that a restored Browns with enhanced tourist appeal could have been integrated into the new shopping street.

At the same time, and just a short distance away, the former yard of the *White Lion Hotel* was still a quiet backwater of old Banbury. In the 18th and 19th centuries the inn had resounded to the clatter of stage-coaches; now tourists came to admire the famous wisteria. During the 1970s the yard was turned into a shopping precinct at the heart of an attractive sequence of passages known as White Lion Walk. In the early years of its life a hot bread shop was a retail honeypot.

The development was small scale compared with some of the ideas that emerged from the Town Development Group based in Oxford. They included the proposal to create a new civic centre close to North Bar and a vision of new unit villages in a ring around Banbury whose target population was to be 70,000. An

131 *The General Foods Factory takes shape in 1965. Nearby Ruscote Avenue still looks like a country lane.*

even larger town of 80,000 was envisaged under the so-called 3D Plan, but Banbury Borough Council voted in favour of more modest growth, to 40,000, though it took the mayor's casting vote to reach this decision.

Towards the end of the 1960s Banbury decided to invest in a new shopping centre. Three competing schemes were put forward, each of which had implications for the town's historical framework. One proposal was to alter substantially the Lanes area of houses and small shops east of St Mary's Church. These alleyways included Tink-a-Tank, which Beesley reckoned gained its name from the sound of receding footsteps on cobbles.[5] A second plan was devised by the Bass/Charrington Group and envisaged a retail complex where the huge Hunt Edmunds Brewery had once stood.

The third, and ultimately successful, scheme was for the redevelopment of a blighted and backland area based on Factory Street and the Castle Streets. Up until the 1950s this had been a much-loved residential fringe of the town centre. During the 19th century there was also

132   *Banbury industry at a glance. General Foods (centre), Automotive Products (opposite), Alcan works (background).*

some industry, notably a rope works. Both Banbury Borough and Oxfordshire County Councils supported a proposal that offered the prospect of covered shopping and national chain stores. Architects led by (Sir) Frederick Gibberd managed to retain the historic frontages to the Market Place and exploit what remained of a corn exchange to create a majestic entry to the malls.

The greatest investment of all has been Castle Quay Shopping Centre. This has polarised retailing within the town but pushed Banbury up the national league table of shopping locations. In 1998 Dun and Bradstreet, well-known analysts, announced that the town was the most prosperous in the United Kingdom. It had the highest proportion of profit-making businesses.

Up until the 1960s it was still possible to find established faces behind counters of family-run shops. Dossett's delicatessen towards the North Bar end of Parsons Street was a classic case. By this time, however, such shops had been joined by the first supermarkets. Fine Fare appeared in Bridge Street and became national news because of the store's expansion behind the preserved frontage of the 19th-century former Baptist chapel. Even the Co-op grocery in Broad Street had changed and become a self-help store from 1949.

By the 1980s pressure was on for stores larger than an historic town centre could accommodate, and after lengthy negotiations with Marlborough Road Methodist Church and Cheneys, the printers, Sainsbury's obtained a site bordering Calthorpe Street. Subsequently

133 *The Mayor, Councillor Fred Blackwell, with developers at the opening of the White Lion shopping precinct.*

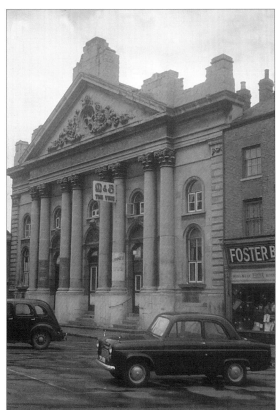

134 *The façade of this former corn exchange became an impressive entrance to the Castle Shopping Centre.*

135 *The Castle Quay, the new commercial heart of Banbury, takes shape.*

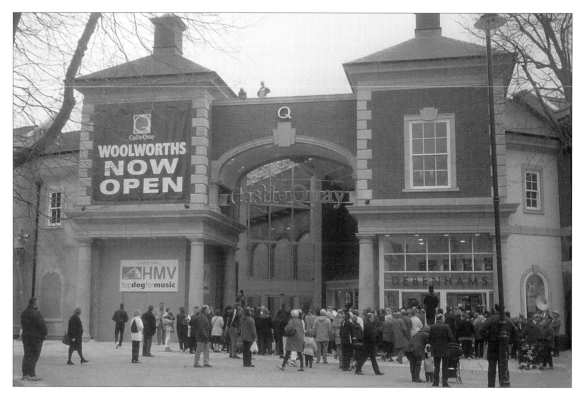

136   *Castle Quay shopping centre entrance: a banner announces Banbury's second coming of Woolworths.*

they moved to a much larger space off the Oxford Road that was sold by Banbury Rugby Club. Tesco appeared in the town a few years later, choosing a position on the Banbury Cross Retail Park close to extensive housing estates and junction 11 of the M40. Morrisons, the last to arrive, preferred former industrial land on the southern edge of the Cherwell area.

This was not the first time retail developments in Banbury had significant consequences for historic buildings. One response back in 1969 was the identification and designation of a conservation area. This is now in urgent need of modification and extension. A county council report about townscape images claimed that 'the centre of the town still retains the basic street plan pattern laid out 1,000 years ago and, with comparatively minor alterations

to accommodate the motor car, the pattern can still form the basis of a thriving town centre, well into the 21st century'.[6] The report established the importance of key views within the historic retail core west of the Market Place. Crucial to such views were Parsons Street, Church Passage and Butchers Row. The town plan of the time reflected these principles.

A combination of regional shopping centre status and access to the relocated museum and tourist information centre has brought new life to Bridge Street and transformed the Oxford Canal corridor. Future proposals for canal zone regeneration south of Bridge Street will incorporate ideas for local transport integration, new style town housing, as well as conservation of a few features of this 19th–century industrial quarter.

137 *A late 1960s townscape image of the Cross end of High Street.*

138 *A late 1960s townscape image incorporating a marina within possible new retail development.*

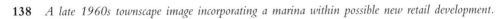

Leisure developments were also a feature of post-war Banbury. In 1956 Ethel Usher, a former licensee of the *White Horse* coaching inn, staged the opening ball of the Winter Gardens in the High Street. This was a collaborative venture with Mr and Mrs Charles Hunt. The venue was built on garden ground formerly occupied by a row of cottages and a lodging house dating to about 1800. Until shortly before the change of use for the land, George Watson, former owner of the property, had used one cottage and an adjacent shed for cultivating mushrooms.

The Winter Gardens dominated the leisure scene in Banbury until its closure in 1982. It was home to a varied range of activities including trade shows, fashion parades, antiques fairs, indoor bowls, boxing, wrestling, roller skating and dancing. Leading national and local bands played there. Victor Sylvester and Brownie Lay were firm favourites.

Apart from the huge number of public houses that had survived from earlier generations, the town's other leisure needs were met until recently by the Palace (Market Place), the Grand (Broad Street) and the Regal (Horse Fair) cinemas, which combined film shows with the opportunity for stage performances. Support in the 1950s and early 1960s was substantial and included patrons from the villages bussed in by local operators such as Sumners of Hornton. The Palace had been a corn exchange, and the Grand assumed an art deco style in the 1930s. But both had screened their last films by 1968 and the Grand was turned into a bingo hall. The Regal survived under a variety of names and has now become a twin-unit Odeon with Dolby sound.

Church House and later the North Oxfordshire College became synonymous with amateur theatrical productions by the Banbury Cross Players, who also used Christ Church Hall in Broad Street for some rehearsals. The Town Hall and the *Crown Hotel* in Bridge Street were popular for dances and Christmas dinners. Wincott's Ballroom in South Bar holds memories for the many devotees of the resident dance band of Ken Prewer.

In 1964, amidst some controversy, Banbury Borough Council built on land historically

140   *Start of an era for Banbury's Winter Gardens.*

141   *The Grand cinema, white building with red drape, is now the Chicago Rock Café.*

known to flood, even though Spiceball Park north of the bridge to Grimsbury had been zoned as public open space on the town map. Their proposals took in some 84 acres of this park, which included part of the Oxford Canal and River Cherwell. Spiceball Park Leisure Centre with its range of wet and dry sports was opened by Sir Roger Bannister in 1974 and extended in 1977 and 1984. Later development included a sports hall that confirmed the popularity of the venue.

Close to Spiceball Park was a building that had been a mill since the 19th century. In 1973 Oxfordshire County Council bought the derelict property and converted it for arts and entertainment. Later conversions included a

small theatre and these made appropriate space for the Mill Drama Group and the various music groups.

In more recent years, especially on weekend evenings, the town centre has become the domain of the young. Nightspots with exotic names such as the Sound Exchange and 52°N have encouraged a move to the 24-hour city concept. The other trend has been the increasing popularity of health and fitness clubs. Often these occupy buildings that were well known in other and earlier contexts. Christ Church School in Grimsbury's Middleton Road and the Co-operative Society shopping arcade off Broad Street are classic examples of part conversion to this use.

142   *The Ken Prewer Band with Brownie Lay on the drums.*

143   *Dancing to the Prewer Band at Wincott's ballroom.*

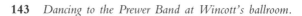

144 *Post-war football euphoria at Spencer Stadium.*

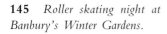

145 *Roller skating night at Banbury's Winter Gardens.*

146   *Health and Fitness Club in the former St Leonard's School, Grimsbury.*

Since the 1970s Banbury has become a more multicultural society. Pioneering men have been joined by their families who, in the case of the Pakistani Muslims, have taken root especially in Grimsbury and particularly in the Causeway. In common with Sikh communities, businesses have been developed right across the town. These include small stores which usually have an emphasis on Asian foods and provision of specialised cuisines. The Muslim Mosque is now well established in Merton Street and the Sikhs have a temple in West Street. The latter is very small and the Sikh community is searching for a suitable location for a temple and community centre. In the town centre places of worship are disappearing where they are redundant or part of a complex of outdated buildings. Recently the Elim church, which occupied the former County Police Station, was bulldozed to make

way for residential infill. The site was just beyond Banbury's conservation area and so lacked any protection.

In 1974 there was a significant turning point in Banbury's affairs. The Borough Council ceased to exist and in its place came a Cherwell district authority. Cherwell District Council embraced Banbury's traditional rival Bicester and stretched southward to the large suburban village of Kidlington, north of Oxford. Inevitably this body has led Banbury in a number of new directions: housing at Hardwick and Bodicote Chase and industrial estates to the north and east of the town. The uniqueness of Banbury continued to be recognised by the Charter Trustees who elected a 'mayor' from amongst the Banbury councillors. In April 2000 Banbury gained a Town Council that has since become based at the mid-19th-century Town Hall.

147 *The old County Police Station (centre) in Newland Road. Another corner of historic Banbury demolished in 2002.*

During the 1980s a different battle was provoked by government proposals to construct the M40 motorway. After it was opened in 1991 a powerful development lobby known as the Cherwell/M40 Investment Partnership began to promote the area, which became increasingly attractive to distribution businesses like Booker Foods. These might have been joined by Coca Cola but local opposition proved too strong. More recently, pavilion-style headquarters of companies such as Alex Lawrie Factors have appeared where medieval fields once gave Banbury's eastern boundary a greener fringe. Some high tech companies such as Vodafone have opted for a more isolated location near Adderbury and known as the Banbury Business Park.

This part of the south Midlands was turned to by house hunters from the Home Counties, many of whom were very affluent by local standards. Their housing needs are altering the face of the area substantially. Edwardian Banbury was a district of large villas with spacious gardens. Current government policies for high-density housing are turning the former into flats and sacrificing the latter so that additional properties can be inserted. This is well illustrated in Dashwood Road.

Some future housing may well follow the lead of retail and business parks by locating outside or close to the 'welcome signs' that remind motorists Banbury is considered an historic market town. Those organisations concerned with the planning of over 1,000 new homes have shown the desire to retain a measure of local and regional identity by their choice of street names.

Village carriers once ensured Banbury was a mecca for the people of the surrounding rural

148   *The M40 has hastened economic development in the Banbury area.*

area. Substantial personal mobility now means that people can reach services beyond the town. Rural inns offer high quality cuisine in traditional village settings. Factory shopping at Bicester Village, garden centres off the Southam Road and in Middleton Cheney, fruit farms and farm shops, and visitor attractions like the National Herb Centre reached by way of the Warwick Road are all examples of reduced dependence on the town itself.

In a major report of 1995,[7] Roger Evans has argued about the need for Banbury to retain its established image as a unique market town with a range of interesting shops and not become just a place with a large indoor shopping centre. Involved in this process is the marketing of historic streets and other spaces so as to foster the sense of a distinctive place. The immediate future must be about what happens to undeveloped areas such as the former Hunt Edmunds Brewery site and the importance of integrating rail, road and possibly canal transport so that Banbury is offered an alternative gateway to that provided by the cluster of buildings at exit 11 on the M40 motorway.

149 *The prospect of substantial housing development on Banbury's southern edge near Bodicote has not gone unchallenged.*

150 *Banbury's Farmers' Market – the future face of produce markets?*

Postscript

This has been a good time to write about Banbury's past as there are still many people living in the town for whom nostalgia is a substitute for a way of life which has all but gone. Before 1998 this revolved around the livestock market. Today and into the foreseeable future it is the motorway that will matter most. This will ensure that an increasingly diverse range of people will look to settle in north Oxfordshire and contribute to a new vibrancy. Very soon a statue of the lady on a white horse will be placed in close proximity to the symbolic cross. Will increased awareness of the 'Ride a Cock Horse' rhyme be sufficient to keep alive ancient traditions or will visitors hurry past in their search for new attractions based on leisure-related shopping? The answer to this question may well determine whether or not the town retains Banburyness.

151   *The Cross and St Mary's Church – essential symbols of Banburyness.*

Notes

Chapter 1: Emergent Banbury

1. Several local writers have used this term, and especially Graham Wilton, a former newspaper editor, for the area that looks to Banbury for goods and services.
2. The term 'Redlands' is derived from the colour of the soil developed on the liassic limestones. A detailed account of the rocks of the area can be found in Edmunds, E.A., Poole, E.G., and Wilson, V., *Geology of the Country around Banbury and Edge Hill* (1965).
3. Numerous ammonites were found in Grimsbury when Thames Water excavated land for a reservoir in the 1960s.
4. The investigation was carried out under the direction of Oxfordshire's archaeologist and his deputy. A private company is processing the results.
5. Trenches were dug in the Calthorpe Street and Calthorpe Gardens areas.
6. Brinkworth, E.R.C., *Old Banbury* (1958), p.1.
7. Beesley, Alfred, *The History of Banbury* (1841), pp.60-2.
8. The reference is in a Pipe Roll E212/81.

Chapter 2: Castles and Church, 1100 to 1500

1. Beesley, Alfred, *The History of Banbury* (1841), pp.63-9.
2. Birmingham University Field Archaeology Unit, *Banbury Town Centre Redevelopment: a Post-excavation assessment and research design*, p.11.
3. Beesley, *The History of Banbury*, p.66 et seq.
4. Johnson, W.P., *A History of Banbury* (*c*.1863).
5. Draper, E. and Potts, W., *The Parish Church, St Mary's Banbury* (1907).
6. Ferris, I., Leach, P. and Litherland, S., 'A Survey of Bridge Street and Mill Lane', *Cake and Cockhorse*, Vol. 12, No. 3 (Summer 1992), pp.54-64.
7. Hardy, A. (ed.), 'The excavation of a Medieval Cottage and Associated Agricultural Features at Manor Farm, Old Grimsbury, Banbury', *Oxoniensia* (2001), pp.345-80.

Chapter 3: Tudor Banbury, 1500 to 1603

1. Church Lane is called Pebble Lane on the map of 1441.
2. The Marches were to the north of the castle.
3. Piccage refers to a toll paid for breaking the ground in setting up booths, stalls, tents, etc. at fairs. Stallage refers to a tax or toll levied for the liberty of erecting a stall in a fair or market.
4. Gibson, J.S.W., 'The Original Banbury Cross', *Cake and Cockhorse*, Vol. 14, No. 8 (Spring 2000), pp.189-97.
5. Richard Corbet was a Bishop of Oxford.

6. Harvey, P., 'Where were Banbury's Crosses?', *Cake and Cockhorse*, Vol. 3, No. 10 (Winter 1967) pp.183-91.
7. Potts made the mistake of thinking there had been a previous cross near the site chosen for the 1859 monument.
8. Beesley, Alfred, *The History of Banbury* (1841), pp.205-10.
9. Gibson, J.S.W. (ed.), *Banbury Wills and Inventories,* Part 1 1591-1620, BHS Vol. 13 (1985), p.26

Chapter 4: Puritans, Civil War and Restoration, 1603 to 1700
1. Gibson, J.S.W., and Brinkworth, E.R.C. (ed.), *Banbury Corporation Records: Tudor and Stuart* BHS Vol. 15 (1977), p.95.
2. *Ibid.*, pp.98-102.
3. Beesley, Alfred, *The History of Banbury* (1841), pp.270-71, quoting from Leigh's 'Epistle Dedicatory to Whateley's Prototypes'.
4. *Ibid.*, pp.278-9.
5. *Ibid.*, p.291.
6. Gibson, J.S.W., 'Trouble over Sheep Pens', *Cake and Cockhorse*, Vol. 7, No. 2 (Spring 1977), pp.35-48.

Chapter 5: The Road to Recovery, 1700 to 1800
1. A detailed description of farming systems can be found in the *Victoria County History for Oxfordshire* Banbury Reprint, pp.49-58.
2. The full list of carriers can be found in *Rusher's Banbury Lists and Directories* (1798-1881)
3. Everitt, A., 'The Primary Towns of England', *Local Historian* Vol.II, No. 5 (Feb. 1975), pp.268-77.
4. Hewitson, C., Hislop, M. and Litherland, S., 'Industrial Archaeological Survey of the Oxford Canal Corridor', Main Summary Report, Birmingham University Field Archaeology Unit Project No. 866 (Nov. 2001).
5. Draper, E. and Potts, W., *The Parish Church, St Mary's Banbury* (1907).
6. Potts, W., *A History of Banbury,* pp.181-2.
7. Renold, P., 'William Rusher: a Sketch of his Life', *Cake and Cockhorse*, Vol. 11, No. 9 (Summer 1991).
8. Potts, W., *Banbury and the Rhyme.*
9. Brinkworth, E.R.C., *Old Banbury* (1958), pp.3-4.
10. Brown-Grant, E., 'The Banbury Horse Races', *Cake and Cockhorse*, Vol. 10, No. 2 (Spring 1986), Vol. 10, No. 3 (Summer 1986), Vol. 10, No. 5 (Spring 1987).
11. Butt, V., 'Banbury Theatre', *Cake and Cockhorse*, Vol. 10, No. 1 (Autumn 1985), pp.12-16, Vol. 10, No. 2 (Spring 1986), pp. 33-6, Vol. 10, No. 4 (Autumn 1986), pp.82-4.

Chapter 6: Growth and Change, 1800 to 1900
1. Rusher, J.G., *Rusher's Banbury Lists and Directories* (1828), p.11.
2. This is recorded in Henderson, W., 'Memoirs' (unpublished).
3. Kinchin-Smith, R., 'Staley's Warehouse', *Cake and Cockhorse,* Vol. 12, Nos. 6/7 (Summer/Autumn 1993), pp.149-71.
4. Hewitson, C., Hislop, M., Litherland, S., *'Industrial Archaeological Survey of the Oxford Canal Corridor'.*
5. Trinder, B., *Victorian Banbury* (1982), p.86.
6. Detailed information about the disposal of Calthorpe Manor land is contained in the Fortesque Papers that are housed in the Centre for Banburyshire Studies of Banbury Library.
7. This map is in the Centre for Oxfordshire Studies, Central Library, Oxford.
8. Potts, W., *A History of Banbury* (1958), p.240.

9. Stated in conveyances of West Bar properties held in the Centre for Oxfordshire Studies, Central Library, Oxford.
10. A copy of an original map for 1882 is held in the Centre for Banburyshire Studies.
11. A copy of *My Life* (1892) can be consulted in the Centre for Banburyshire Studies.
12. Draper, E., *Gleams of interest across the Parish Church Chimes of St Mary's, Banbury* (1901).

Chapter 7: The Market Town Diversifies, 1900 to 1945

1. Gibson, J.S.W., 'The Immediate Route from the Metropolis to All Parts', *Cake and Cockhorse*, Vol. 12, No. 1 (1991), pp.10-24.
2. Dossett-Davies, J.W., '**From a North Bar Window – a child's view of Banbury in the 1930s**', *Cake and Cockhorse*, Vol. 13, No. 3 (1995), pp.89-98.
3. Miller, Rev. G., in letters to *Banbury Guardian* (January 1901).
4. Morland, B.R. (pub.), *Guide to Banbury and District* (1901).
5. Little, B.E., *Changing Faces of Banbury* (1998).
6. The details of changes in Bridge Street are recorded in the minute books of Banbury Charities.
7. Little, *Changing Faces*.
8. Today several different charitable bodies are grouped under the title of Banbury Charities.
9. Hodgkins, J.R., *Over the Hills to Glory* (1978) contains a detailed account of the industrial unrest at the Northern Aluminium Company.
10. E.W., *The Pathways of Banburyshire* (1900) gives descriptions of these walks.
11. Williams Orchard's observations about the Crooked Shades are made in a letter to Banbury Corporation dated 5 March 1904, which is part of a private collection of Orchard letters.

Chapter 8: Post-War Developments 1945–2002

1. Davis, B. and Little, B.E., *The Changing Faces of Easington* (2000), p.55.
2. *The Farmers' Weekly*, Vol. XLVII, No. 6 (1957), p.65.
3. *Banbury Guardian*, Nostalgia Column, 14 June 2001.
4. Wright, M., 'The Penalties of Indifference', *Country Life*, 9 May 1968, pp.1, 201.
5. Town Development Group, *Banbury Seventy Thousand*, Oxfordshire County Council (1966).
6. Opher, Philip and Campbell, Stefania (eds.), *Conservation Study No. 2: Banbury*, Oxfordshire County Council (undated, ?1968).
7. Roger Evans Associates and Hillier Parker, *Urban Design Strategies: Banbury: Bicester: Kidlington,* report to Cherwell District Council (undated, ?1966).

BIBLIOGRAPHY

General

The Agricultural Economics Research Institute, Oxford, *County Planning* (1944)

Allen, Peter, *Cherwell Valley Railway: The Social History of an Oxfordshire Railway* (1999)

Banbury Historical Society Records:

  Banbury Wills and Inventories: Part 1 1591-1620, Vol. 13 (1985)

  Banbury Corporation Records: Tudor and Stuart, Vol. 15 (1977)

  The Bawdy Court of Banbury, Vol. 26 (1997)

Cake and Cockhorse, the magazine of the Banbury Historical Society issued to members three times a year

Beesley, Alfred, *The History of Banbury* (1841)

Bloxham, C., *The Book of Banbury* (1975)

Brinkworth, E.R.C., *Old Banbury* (1958)

Draper, E., *Notes on Calthorpe Manor House, Banbury* (1915)

Draper, E., *Gleams of Interest Across the Parish Church Chimes of St Mary's* (1901)

Draper, E. and Potts, W., *The Parish Church St Mary's Banbury* (1907)

Evans, Roger and Opher, Philip, 'Making Places: High Street, Banbury', *The Architect's Journal*, 22, IV (1992)

Herbert, G., *Shoemaker's Window* (1948)

Johnson, W., *The History of Banbury* (1863)

Little, B., *The Changing Faces of Banbury* (1998)

Little, B., *The Changing Faces of Grimsbury* (1999)

Little, B. and Davis, B., *The Changing Faces of Easington* (2000)

Mann, Michael, *Workers on the Move* (1973)

Opher, Philip and Campbell, Stefania (eds), *Conservation Study No 2: Banbury, Oxon*, The County Architect, Oxon C.C. (undated, ?1968)

Pearson, E., *Banbury Chapbooks* (1970)

Potts, W., *Banbury Through a Hundred Years* (1942)

Potts, W., *A History of Banbury* (1958)

Roger Evans Associates and Hillier Parker, *Urban Design Strategies: Banbury, Bicester, Kidlington*, report to Cherwell District Council

Rusher, J.G., *Rusher's Banbury Lists and Directories* (1797-1881)

Stacey, M., *Tradition and Change: A Study of Banbury* (1960)

Stacey, M., Batstone, E. and Bell, C., *Power, Persistence and Change* (1975)

Town Development Group, *Banbury Seventy Thousand* (1966)

Trinder, B., *Victorian Banbury* (1982)

Victoria County History of Oxfordshire

Wood, V., *The Licensees of the Inns, Taverns and Beerhouses of Banbury, Oxfordshire* (1998)

INDEX

Figures in **bold** indicate page numbers of illustrations